ONLY THE BEST

*Fantastic International Recipes
With A Regional Flair*

*by Colonel John J. Koneazny
and his Good Wife Dottie*

ILLUSTRATED BY CHRIS LINCOLN

R & E PUBLISHERS

R&E Publishers
P.O. Box 2008, Saratoga, CA 95070
Tel: (408) 866-6303   Fax: (408) 866-0825

Book design and Typesetting by elletro Productions

Book Cover & Illustrations by Chris Lincoln

ISBN   1-56875-051-X

Designed, typeset and totally manufactured in the
United States of America.

Introduction

Must say the prospect of writing an introduction to a cookbook by the fayaway Captain and Mate never crossed my mind on occasions of Waterway reunions in one port or another. Renee and I always thought their library of sea chanties and other scurrilous musical verse deserved archival treatment. However, we know the core of Jack's music library so painstakingly preserved by Dottie, the legendary record keeper, was stolen from their station wagon on one of their annual migrations from Massachusetts to Georgia or Florida. The music went with the beloved Autoharp.

The recipe collection did survive the burglary; and here we are about to savor the tastes, the enthusiasms of Jack and Dottie's kitchen or barbecue ashore and their galley in Fayaway on the Waterway, the Bahamas, the Keys, and the Gulf Coast. The gusto with which they would whip up the edibles required to satisfy the hunger of unexpected guests, and the strategy of planning bigger feasts for hungry hordes of yacht people and the shoreside support troops amazed us on the scene, now delights us with its seasoning of this chronicle.

The first time we met, in Savannah at the Isle of Hope Marina, I found myself helping them down the gangway with the first of many cartloads of supplies that had their venerable ark of a station wagon perilously overweight. Getting their homemade venison sausage out of dry ice storage into a proper freezer of a land person was the most critical part of logistics. To get frozen and chilled goodies safely down to FAYAWAY required an Enduro drive straight thru from Massachusetts, a driving feat we have seen exceeded by them many times since.

They have never, however, to the best of our knowledge missed a meal in their travels. Somehow they manage to include a chow stop as required, the details recorded for the benefit of their friends, the grateful recipients of the Christmas travel bulletins. Now you, with this spirited cookbook in hand, can share the light-hearted ebullience of the Koneazny hospitality routine. Enjoy!

Kirby Atterbury

Atterbury Letter, Wine-Dining-Travel
P. 0. Box 1197
Bethel Island, CA 94511

We have many international recipes in this book, so I thought I'd get you in the mood by having a fiesta.

Dishes from:

United States

Canada	Germany
Bahamas	Corsica
Jamaica	Malta
Thailand	Near East
Russia	Poland
Ireland	Greece
England	Switzerland
Spain	Haiti
France	India
Italy	Turkey
Indonesia	Scotland
Senegal	

WE'LL GUIDE YOU THROUGH OUR
COOK BOOK, ALONG WITH HELPERS
PEDRO PEPPER AND STALKY
STRINGBEAN.

Foreword

What! Another cookbook? Why, and why by you?

Yes, there are thousands of cookbooks on the market, but how many do you use? How many have you chucked out or given away? How many are sitting on your cookbook shelf - some not opened in over a year?

Well, I know, I have plenty! There might be one or two recipes in each book I like, then when my wife, Dottie, says, "Let's have Hawaiian Chicken cooked in coconut shells", which book holds the recipe?

We decided to put all the recipes we liked in a loose leaf notebook for easy reference. When we went to someone's home for dinner and had an outstanding dish, we came home with the recipe and it went into the "notebook". On trips abroad or to restaurants in this country, if we couldn't get the recipe we went home and tried to duplicate it in our kitchen. When we thought we had it, into the notebook it went. Over the years it grew to its present size and many of our friends asked us to publish.

Well, at first I didn't take the suggestions very seriously, but one day, while looking through the "notebook" for a dinner menu, I thought it wouldn't take much work to get it in shape.

Back we went through the recipes and put amounts in most of them. (Where I don't have the exact amount of an ingredient, add a little at a time until it tastes good to you.)

I come from a long line of excellent amateur chefs. My mother and father were well known locally for their culinary abilities. My Irish grandmother always cooked for a crowd and produced some wonderful meals. Both of my brothers and their wives are good cooks, and brother Bill ran a gourmet catering business for many years.

Food and methods of preparation have always been an important part of my life.

I love to invent new dishes, only using a recipe as a guide line. I cook by tasting and build my dishes by what's on hand. If I don't have an ingredient, I'll try another and had many pleasant surprises along with a few flops!

We can't remember a guest in recent years leaving out table without a compliment to the chef and many times it's "The best I've ever tasted".

This is not a gourmet cookbook. The dishes are mostly easy to prepare and should not be a problem to anyone with basic kitchen know-how.

"Only The Best" starts with an easy reference to herbs and spices, a section on how to substitute if you don't have an ingredient on hand and an article on low calorie cooking.

In the back of the book you will find sections pertaining to Kitchen Know-How, Temperature Conversions and Weights and Measures.

There is a section, "A Menu Log". This is handy if your memory is as poor as mine. "What did we serve the last time the Jones's were here, we don't want to give them the same thing, again?" "I don't remember, but it's in the log", my loyal spouse replies.

Another section lets you record dietary needs and preferences of frequent guests. Here you can record what they drink, like and dislikes in food, calorie, cholesterol and sodium requirements if any. Guests will really think they are special when you say, "Joe, do you still drink Mount Gay Rum and soda with lime juice and does Mary still drink Southern Comfort?"

There is also a section to list your own favorite dishes.

After many of the recipes there is a list of variations. This feature almost doubles the material for your choices.

There are suggested ways to prepare dishes with ingredients you would rather use or have on hand. They may also give you ideas to slightly change leftovers to add variety for your family.

As Dottie and I have spent the last eighteen winters living on a sailboat, many of the dishes are one pot simple meals that can be stove-top cooked, so this would be a good book to carry on a boat or in an RV. or to use at your vacation place. There are recipes from 27 different countries plus regional dishes from New England, the South, some Cajun and the far west of this country.

Dottie and I have traveled to most of these places and have returned with a tape recorder full of menus and recipes. We hope you have as much pleasure trying these meals as we have had.

Well, that's about it, if you like the book let me know through the publisher and be good to others, be happy and have a good life!

Jack Koneazny
Sheffield, MA. 01257

Contents

Sauces

APPETIZERS

HAMBURGER, SAUSAGE AND LIVER

Herbs and Spices

Herbs and spices are of course the most important "secret" ingredient in producing gourmet food.

Remember that herbs and spices deteriorate with age so you may have to use more than the recipe calls for if the seasoning is old.

If your storage space is small combine herbs and spices such as curry powder, Italian seasoning, bouquet garni, chili powder and the like will save a little room.

When first experimenting with herbs use a little at a time. Seasonings like rosemary can completely over power a dish with even a teaspoon of the dried herb. Many people won't eat food that is spicy hot.

Soups and stews should have herbs added in the last hour of cooking.

Quick cooking dishes should have the herbs added early in the cooking.

Cold mixes such as refrigerated dips should steep for hours.

Here are the most common seasonings and the dishes and cuisine they are usually used with:

Allspice   Marinades, soup, spice cakes and pickling. A West Indian seed which could be said to have the flavor of cinnamon, cloves, nutmeg and mace. Hence the name.

Anise   Sauces, confectionery, cakes, liqueurs and Far Eastern cooking. (see Chinese Duck)

Basil   Italian, Spanish, Greek and French recipes. Tomatoes, cold salads, pesto sauce, marinara sauce, etc.

Bay Leaf   Soups, stews, marinades, sauces and game. Used in French and Italian cooking. Bay leaves should be removed before serving.

Capers   Mediterranean cooking, sauces, tomatoes, eggplant, beef and veal. Capers are unopened flower buds picked at night. They are packed in vinegar or salt.

Caraway   Cheeses, sauerkraut, rye bread, Cole slaw, beets, potatoes, cakes and cookies. Used in Scandinavian cooking.

Cardamom   Scandinavian and German cooking, pastries, vegetables and curry powder.

Cassia   Use as cinnamon. It has a stronger taste but less aroma.

Cayenne   A hot red pepper used in many dishes.

Celery Seed	A substitute for fresh celery. Used in thousands of dishes such as soups, stews, seafood, hamburger and vegetables. Celery salt is a mixture of ground seed and salt. Great for Bloody Mary's.
Chervil	Use with cottage cheese, fish, egg dishes, vegetables and soups.
Chili Powder	A mixture of spices which may contain paprika, cumin, cayenne, garlic and/or oregano. Used in chili con carne and other Mexican dishes.
Chives	The green leaves and stalk of a grass like, delicate member of the onion family. Use as onion. Great for cottage cheese, sour cream and dips.
Cinnamon	Desserts, fruit, pickling, fish, stews, rice pudding, French toast, hot buttered rum, etc.
Cloves	Hams, onions, pickles, sauerbraten, sweets, spareribs, etc. One of the most important of all the spices.
Coriander	Far Eastern cooking, curries, soups, stews, celery. Use sparingly.
Cumin	Mexican, Indian, Spanish and Italian cuisine. Chili powder, curry powder. Use sparingly.
Curry Powder	A mixture of spices used extensively in Indian and Far Eastern cooking. Soups, lamb, seafood, chicken, eggs and fruit. Turmeric, mustard, allspice, cardamom, coriander, pepper, cloves, mace, ginger and etc. are the spices used. Two basic formulations are Bombay and Madris curry powder.
Dill	Dips, pickles, eggs, seafood, meat, potatoes, cucumbers, sour cream, breads, etc.
Fennel	Sausage, Italian and French cooking, fish, vegetables, chicken, soups, salads and etc. The celery like plant is used as a vegetable. Tastes a little like anise.
Fenugreek	An ingredient of curry powder.
File	Creole dishes such as gumbo. File gumbo powder is a blend of sassafras leaves and dried okra.
Garlic	Provincial French, Southern Italian, Mexican and Mediterranean cooking. Meat, seafood, fondue, eggplant, tomatoes, spaghetti sauce, salads and etc.

Ginger	Chinese cooking, desserts, fruit and meat. Canton ginger is milder than Jamaica ginger.
Horseradish	Cocktail sauce, tongue, boiled beef and dips. Very hot when fresh, but looses strength quickly. Keep refrigerated.
Juniper Berry	Venison, stews, lamb, game marinades.
Mace	Fruits, desserts and pickles. Milder but similar to nutmeg.
Marjoram	Sauces, soups, stews, stuffing, lamb, sausage and vegetables.
Mint	Carrots, peas, jelly, lamb, desserts and tea.
Mustard Seed	(powder) Roast meat, seafood, sauces, pickles and salad dressings. Prepared mustard can be used in any recipe calling for the seed or powder.
Nutmeg	Desserts, eggnog, cheese dishes, eggs and custards. Buy whole nutmegs and grate it when needed. They will keep for years. The grated nutmeg deteriorates rapidly.
Oregano	Used in Italian, Spanish and Mexican cooking. Also in tomato sauce, pizza, eggplant and chicken.
Paprika	Hungarian dishes. Goulash, chicken and garnishing. The Spanish variety is hot and the Hungarian paprika is mild. Buy good quality as the low priced has the flavor of sawdust.
Parsley	Garnishes, potatoes, herb bread, vegetables and salads. Dried, the herb looses most of its flavor.
Pepper	The most commonly used spice in the world.
Black Pepper	Malabar, Lampon, Penang and black peppers from the places indicated.
White Pepper	Black pepper with the hull removed. Used in white sauces and light colored dishes.
Jamaica Pepper	Allspice.
Chili Pepper	Red peppers such as bird, devil, Tabasco, cayenne - very hot.

Nepal and Creole Peppers	Yellow peppers.
Poppy Seed	Noodles, pastries, bread and dips.
Rosemary	Stuffing, biscuits, chicken, meat loaf and etc. Use sparingly.
Saffron	Italian, Spanish and Mediterranean cooking. Paella, rice, chicken and etc. This is the herb that gives yellow rice its color. A small pinch is usually all you need and can afford. If you ever get to Turkey, buy it at about 1/5th the price.
Sage	Sausage, poultry, pork, veal, cheese and stuffing.
Savory	Poultry, fish, peas, beans and salads.
Sesame	Pastry, rolls, bread, Chinese and Near East cooking. Comes as seeds, paste and oil.
Tarragon	French cooking. Chicken, veal, fish, potatoes, vinegar.
Thyme	Caribbean cooking. Chowder, soups, stews, onions, stuffing and fish. Use sparingly.
Turmeric	Curries and pickles. This spice gives a yellow color to curries and pickles.
Vanilla	Ice cream, cakes, puddings and cookies.

Substitutions

These recipes will call for an ingredient which perhaps are not on the shelf. By all means substitute! Here are some examples of substitutions that are commonly used in the culinary profession.

Champagne   mix ginger ale with a little cider vinegar.

Shallots   boil garlic in water with a little sugar added for a few minutes.

Chili powder   mix 25 parts paprika with 8 parts cumin and 1 part cayenne pepper.

Curry powder   (Bombay) mix 8 parts turmeric with 7 parts coriander, 4 parts fenugreek, 2 parts each of mustard, cinnamon and ginger and 1 part each of cloves, mace and black pepper.

Curry powder   (Madras) mix 8 parts each of coriander, turmeric and cumin, 4 each of black pepper and ginger, 2 each of fenugreek, cardamom, cayenne pepper and mace-and 1 each of mustard and cloves. Garlic - Use the powder or salt when fresh is not on hand.

Chives   Use green onion tops minced or even a little suggestion of minced onion.

Celery   Use celery seed.

Anchovies   Use the paste.

Oregano   Mix a little sage and thyme.

Fennel   Mix celery, dill and anise seed.

Chicken   When dishes call for chicken, substitute with Cornish game hens, turkey or pheasant.

Ketchup   Tomato soup with vinegar and sugar.

Sweet wine   Add sugar to dry wine.

Oil   All cooking oils and animal fats are interchangeable. When olive oil is called for chop an olive and sauté in the oil.

Butter	Cooking oil and butter flavored salt.
Flour	Cornstarch.
Herb vinegars	Add the dried herb to the dish while cooking.
Game birds	Doves, quail, marsh hens, grouse, etc. can be interchanged in recipes.
Salt	Soy sauce or bouillon.

Low Calorie Cooking

Being one of those unfortunate people who gain a pound every time I walk by a food store, I am always looking for ways to cut calories. There are many, many ways to loose weight and most of them, believe it or not, work if you stick with them. The hard thing is of course to be always on a diet. All of the experts agree that it is better to cut down on a well balanced diet than try the current fad whether it be fruit, carbohydrate, low fat or whatever.

The recipes in this book can be made lower in calories with a little common sense. There are many diet aids on the market that are really a boom to those trying to loose pounds.

1. When a recipe calls for frying in three tablespoons oil or butter, use three tablespoons diet margarine and cut 150 calories. Better yet, use one of the no calorie sprays, such as Pam, Weight Watchers, etc.

2. Where sugar is called for (except for baking) try artificial sweeteners. NutraSweet, while expensive, does not have the bitter taste of saccharin.

3. Don't worry about wine or other spirits in a recipe as the alcohol will evaporate during cooking and that's where the calories are.

4. Use skim milk where a recipe calls for whole milk.

5. Imitation sour cream and cream cheese will save calories.

6. When making gravies use less fat and flour and make a lighter gravy.

7. Trim the fat off meat before cooking.

8. Try a salad dressing without oil. Mix vinegar, water and lemon juice with plenty of seasoning.

9. There is a low calorie butter substitute called "Butter Buds" in the diet section of most grocery stores. This is mixed with water and can be used on potatoes, rice, noodles and vegetables. Used dry it can be used on popcorn for a low calorie snack.

10. When deep frying, use light batter (see Page 29)

11. Use egg beaters or the like for replacement in recipes that call for eggs. No cholesterol and about 40% less calories per egg.

12. Use low cal bread for sandwiches, French toast, etc.

13. When stir frying, add water to the pan in place of oil.

14. Serve more broiled fish.

15. Skin chicken before cooking.

16. When serving snacks always put out a plate of veggies with a low cal dip.

17. When making soups and stews always skim off the fat.

18. Drink 12 ounces of water shortly before you eat.

19. Serve low cal desserts such as fresh fruit and diet puddings.

20. Substitute ground turkey for hamburger, in burgers, chili or meatloafs or mix half and half.

Do what I say if you want to be as good looking as me.

DRINKS

Homemade Kahlua
from Charles Henry, Savannah, GA.

4 cups sugar
2 oz. instant coffee
2 cups boiling water

1 Vanilla bean
2 cups vodka

Blend sugar, coffee and boiling water. Cool to room temperature. Add vodka. Suspend a vanilla bean in container. Close lid tightly and set in refrigerator for 30 days. Shake container occasionally.

Makes one quart

Homemade Creme de Menthe

from Flo Wheaton, Florida Keys

1-1/2 cups vodka
1/2 t. peppermint extract
2 t. vanilla extract

1-1/4 cups basic syrup*
Few drops green food coloring

Combine all ingredients. Store in a tight lid jar for at least one week.

* Basic syrup: One lemon, 2 cups water, 3 cups granulated sugar. Pare yellow of outside of lemon (no white). Blot on paper towel to remove oil. Combine sugar, water and heat in saucepan. Heat to boiling. Lower heat and simmer 5 minutes.
Strain and cool to room temperature.

Makes about one quart

Irish Creme Liqueur

1 cup Irish whiskey
1 can (14 oz.) Eagle Brand Condensed Milk
4 Eggs
2 t. Vanilla Extract

2 t. Chocolate extract
1 t. Coconut extract
1 t. powdered instant expresso
(regular coffee can be substituted)

Put all above ingredients in blender. Chill.

Toasted Hazelnut Liqueur

6-1/2 oz. peeled toasted hazelnuts, chopped
2-1/2 cups boiling water 2-1/2 cups vodka
1/2 vanilla bean or 2 T. pure vanilla extract
3/4 cup sugar

Put the hazelnuts into a 6 cup glass jar or container. Pour the boiling water over them. Let cool completely. Add the vodka and the vanilla. Let steep for approximately two weeks in the refrigerator.
Remove one-third of the mixture from the jar. In it dissolve all the sugar, then add this to the bulk of the infusion. Let age for several months.
Filter through a coffee filter and store in one or two well-sealed bottles.

Homemade Galliano

1 qt. water
2 cups sugar
1 oz. Strega

Boil five minutes until light syrup then add:

1/2 bottle Anisette
1/2 t. pure vanilla extract
4 cups vodka

Mix well, you just saved yourself over $15.00!

Mocha Punch

1 small jar instant coffee
1 can chocolate syrup
3 quarts milk

1 pint boiling water
1 quart vanilla ice cream

Dissolve instant coffee in boiling water. Add syrup and mix well. Add remaining ingredients.
About 30 cups

Georgia Peach Soup

Here is a Dixie recipe that can be used as a dessert or goes great while sitting under the magnolia tree on a hot summer afternoon.

2 pints half and half
4 T. honey
1 nutmeg, grated
3 t. cinnamon

2 oz. Amaretto
1 oz. dark rum
6 ripe peaches, skinned
Fresh mint

Whip half and half until stiff. Add all ingredients to a food processor or blender and mix until peaches are liquefied. Garnish with mint. 4 servings

Variations

Rum my be omitted or more added according to preference.

Instant Russian Tea Mix

1/2 cup instant tea
2 cups orange Tang
1-1/2 cups sugar

1 t. cinnamon
1/2 t. ground cloves
1/2 t. dry lemon rind

Mix well. Use about 2-1/2 teaspoons to a cup of boiling water.

Cappuccino Mix

1/2 cup instant coffee
3/4 cup sugar
1 cup dry milk

3/4 t. dried orange peel
Pinch ot baking soda

Mix well and use two to three teaspoons in a cup of boiling water.

Deluxe Mexican Chocolate

4 oz. unsweetened chocolate
4 cups milk
2 cups cream
6 T. sugar

Pinch of nutmeg and allspice
2 t. cinnamon
2 eggs
2 t. vanilla

Grate chocolate in top of double boiler over boiling water. Add 1/2 cup boiling water and heat until smooth. Stir in hot milk, cream, sugar and spices. Cook an hour, beating vigorously every ten minutes. When ready to serve, beat eggs with vanilla, add a little of the hot chocolate to eggs then stir into the remaining chocolate. Beat vigorously several minutes and serve at once in hot mugs.

Daiquiri Slush

2 oz. rum
3/4 cup powdered sugar
1 6 oz. can frozen concentrate lemonade

2 egg whites
3 cups crushed ice

Put all ingredients in blender. Blend at high speed until it turns to slush. Freeze for 2 hours.

Makes 3 to 4 servings

Shipboard Sangria

1/2 gal. red wine
1 16 oz. can orange juice
4 oz. fresh or bottled lemon juice
Grated lemon rind

1/2 cup sugar
Chopped fresh fruit
1 qt. club soda

Mix in pitcher with lots of ice. Add club soda just before serving.

Variations

1. Use ginger ale in place of club soda.
2. Use lime juice instead of the lemon juice.
3. You can lower the calories by using NutraSweet in place of the sugar.

Hot Mulled Wine

fathers drank to ward off the chill blanes on cold winter evenings. Great
ile party as with the two following drinks:

1 t. whole cloves
3 cinnamon sticks

ices to boil and simmer for 10 minutes. Cool slightly and add wine and

Hot Buttered Rum

2 oz. dark rum
Freshly grated nutmeg

in a warm mug and fill with boiling water.

Variations

be added to each serving.
in each cup for a stirrer.

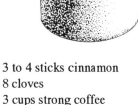

Cafe Brulot

1 cup brandy
8 lumps sugar
Peel of an orange

3 to 4 sticks cinnamon
8 cloves
3 cups strong coffee

Make coffee. Use a bowl that can be heated and get it hot. Peel orange in one long spiral ribbon. Put peel, spices and 6 lumps of sugar in bowl. Add brandy. dip up some brandy in a ladle. Add remaining sugar lumps and ignite. Pour back and forth burning peel and remaining sugar. Slowly add coffee and as the flame flickers ladle into cups.

4 servings

Gun Club Punch

1 oz. dark rum
1 oz. light rum
1/2 oz. orange liqueur

1 oz. lime juice
1 T. sugar
Cracked ice

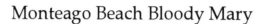

Blend in blender 4 or 5 seconds or shake in cocktail shaker. Serve in a tall glass.

1 serving

Monteago Beach Bloody Mary

I picked this one up from the bartender at the Monteago Beach Hotel. He wouldn't tell me his secret, so I had to order enough of them to learn by observing.

6 oz. tomato juice
1-1/2 oz. vodka
3 T. Ketchup
Celery salt to taste

1 t. sugar
Pickapepper or Tiger Sauce to taste
2 t. lime juice
Cut fresh lime

Put all the above ingredients in a glass, stir well, add ice, lime and serve.

Makes one ten oz. serving

First Artillery Punch

For Christmas, New Years or the 4th of July. Here is a wonderful punch that will make you the toast of the town. Very explosive!

1 lb. loaf sugar (use granular if loaf not available)
3 lemons
2 oranges
1 qt. champagne

1 qt. Jamaica dark rum
1 qt. sherry
1/2 pint brandy
1 qt. black and green tea (mixed)

Put sugar in punch bowl. Grate upon it rinds of 3 lemons and juice of 2 oranges. Add boiling tea. Stir, then cool, cover. When cool add rum, then the sherry and the brandy stirring slowly all the while. Set punch bowl in a bed of crushed ice. Just before serving add the champagne.

Makes 18 to 22 four oz. drinks

Yellow Bird

The official drink of the Caribbean.

2 oz. orange juice	1 oz. light rum
1 oz. lemon juice	1/2 oz. apricot brandy
1/2 oz. simple syrup	1/2 oz. banana liqueur

Mix above ingredients together and shake well. Serve in tall glass with ice cubes. Add orange slice and cherry.

1 serving

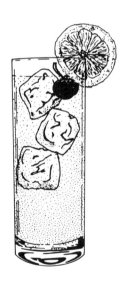

SAUCES AND STOCKS

Sauce Béchamel (white sauce)

Melt 4 T. butter in a sauce pan. Remove from heat and add 4 T. flour stirring all the while until well blended. Add slowly 2 cups of milk room temperature stirring constantly. Return to heat and add a little salt and white pepper and cook until sauce thickens.

Makes 2 cups

Quick Béchamel Sauce

1 onion, chopped
1 pint milk
1 Bay leaf

Pinch of mace, clove, sage and thyme
1 t. granulated gelatin
1/4 t. chicken bouillon

Simmer onion and spices in milk for 15 minutes. Strain into a bowl and add gelatin. Melt 1 T. butter and add 1 T. flour and make a white roux. Work in the seasoned milk and simmer a few minutes longer.

Morney Sauce

Add 2 T. Gruyere and 2 T. Parmesan cheese freshly grated to 2 cups of rich Béchamel sauce. Heat in a double boiler.

Easy Béarnaise Sauce

2 T. white wine
1 T. tarragon vinegar
2 t. chopped tarragon
2 t. chopped shallots or onion

1/4 t. salt and pepper
1/2 cup butter
3 egg yolks
2 T. lemon juice

Combine wine vinegar, tarragon, shallots and pepper in a pan. Cook rapidly until almost all the liquid is gone. In a small sauce pan, heat butter until bubbling but not brown.

In an electric blender, put yolks, lemon juice and salt. Flip on to high and then off. Turn motor on high and gradually add hot butter. Add herb vinegar mixture and blend for 4 seconds.

Makes about 1 cup

Court Bouillon

Put into a large pot 8 cups water, 4 cups dry white wine, 3 large onions, chopped, 3 celery stalks with leaves, chopped, 5 T. chopped parsley, 1/2 t. thyme, 2 bay leaves, 8 white peppercorns, cracked and 1 T. salt. Bring to a boil and simmer for about 1 hour. Cool and strain.

Used for poaching fish and shellfish.

Makes 2 quarts

Seasoned Butter

Garlic, parsley, tarragon, basil, dill, thyme, horseradish and Worcestershire sauce can be added to butter creamed with a little lemon juice. Add a little freshly ground pepper. Chill if possible.

Herb butter

1 t. chives, tarragon, 2 t. parsley, salt and pepper.

Clarified Butter

Dipping butter for seafood is much nicer if clarified. Melt butter in double boiler over low heat. Pour off the clear butter and discard the thin liquid.

Hollandaise Sauce

Combine three egg yolks, 1/4 cup of cold water, 2 T. lemon juice and a little cayenne pepper in the top of a double boiler. Beat with a wooden spoon or a whisk until smooth. Divide 4 T. butter into 3 parts and add one part to egg yolks. Place over hot water. Cook stirring all the while until the butter melts. Do the same with the second portion and then the third, and cook until sauce thickens.

Makes 3/4 of a cup

Easy Hollandaise Sauce

For shipboard or camper use, I strongly urge the packaged Hollandaise Sauce sold **by** French, McCormick and others. While they are not as good as homemade, they save time and space and do not curdle.

If you want to do it from scratch you will need a double boiler.

White Wine Fish Stock

2 lb. fish heads and bones
4 T. oil
1 onion, chopped
2 carrots, sliced
2 ribs celery, sliced
4 cups white wine

4 cups water
Pinch of fennel
5 sprigs parsley
1 bay leaf
Salt and pepper to taste

Heat oil. Cook vegetables until they start to color. Add wine, water and fish. Bring to a boil, then skim. Add spices and simmer for several hours. Strain.

Variation

A passable substitute can be made in a hurry with fish bouillon, wine, water and the vegetables and spices listed above and simmered for about 30 minutes.

Anchovy Sauce

Dissolve 2 t. anchovy paste in one cup of melted butter. Stir in 1/4 cup sherry. Heat to simmer and cook for 5 minutes.

Barbecue Sauces

There are as many barbecue sauces as there are cooks. You should experiment and when you find what you like, record it in the blank space below. If it's real good bottle it and make a fortune!

Try mix and match with the following:

1 cup	Ketchup or tomato soup or tomato sauce or canned tomatoes.
2 T. prepared	Mustard - dry, seed, Chinese, spicy or with horseradish.
1/4 cup	Vinegar, cider, red wine, tarragon, rice or lemon juice.
1 to 4 T.	Sugar - white, brown, honey, syrup or low cal.
1/3 cup	Onion - minced, mashed, juice, powder or salt.
1 to 4 cloves	Garlic - minced, mashed, juice, powder or salt.
2 T. to 1/2 cup	Fat - butter, margarine or oil.
To taste	Spices - chili powder, ginger or nutmeg.
To taste	Salt - seasoned salt, soy sauce or bouillon.
To taste	Pepper black, red, Tiger Sauce, Pickapeppa or Tabasco.
To taste	Other—Worcestershire, Al, fruit, wine, brandy, bourbon, gin or beer.

Charles Henry's Barbecue Sauce

Charles Henry who travels many, many miles per year brought this back from New Orleans. He went right into the kitchen of large hotel to obtain this simple but delicious sauce.

    2 10 oz. bottles Heinz Chili Sauce
    1 1 lb. can cranberry sauce

Mix and simmer down until smooth. Can be served with poultry, ribs, beef, fish or most anything you want finger lickin' good. Use on chicken, turkey, game hens or duck.

Caper Sauce

Add 1/4 cup of capers to 1 cup of Drawn Butter Sauce.

Cardinal Sauce

To a pint of béchamel sauce, add 2 T. of red lobster eggs. Take from the fire and stir in 1 T. lobster butter.

Cheese Sauces

Heat Velvetta type cheese (1/2 lb.) with 1/4 cup of milk and 1/2 t. prepared mustard. Heat 1/2 cup of milk with 8 oz. cream cheese, 2 oz. blue cheese and 1/4 t. onion powder.

Cucumber Sauce

Combine 1 t. grated onion with 3 T. sour cream, 1/2 cup grated cucumber, 1 t. salt, 1/2 t. prepared mustard and 1 T. vinegar. Let marry in refrigerator several hours if possible.

Cucumber Sauce for Fish

To the above, add 1/2 cup chopped cucumbers and 3 T. chopped onions. Omit Worcestershire sauce.

Cumberland Sauce

Melt in a double boiler, 1/4 pint of currant jelly. Add an equal amount of port wine. Add the juice of an orange and lemon and a little pepper. Do not boil but keep warm for 15 minutes before serving. Use on venison or other game.

Easy Curry Sauce

1 cup sour cream
1/4 cup mayonnaise

1-1/2 t. curry powder
Chopped green onions

Blend all ingredients.

Drawn Butter Sauce

Blend 3 T. flour with 3 T. of melted butter. Add 1/4 t. salt and pepper. Stir in 1-1/2 cups hot water and boil for 5 minutes. Mix in 4 T. of butter, a little at a time, and 1 t. of lemon juice.

Horseradish Sauce

1/4 cup butter
1/4 cup flour

2 cups beef broth
2 to 3 T. horseradish

Melt butter in sauce pan, add flour and whisk until smooth. Bring broth to boil and add the beef broth all at once to the flour, whisk vigorously. Simmer 5 minutes and add the horseradish and serve hot. Great on corned beef!

Mayonnaise Sauce for Fish

1/2 cup mayonnaise
1/2 cup sour cream
1 t. dill weed, minced

Worcestershire sauce to taste
Salt and pepper to taste
2 T. parsley, chopped

Combine all ingredients. This can be put over fish and baked for a delicious dish or used from the table on baked or broiled fish. Let flavors marry in refrigerator several hours.

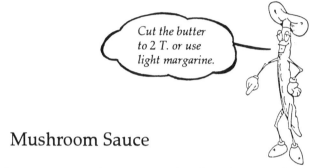

Cut the butter to 2 T. or use light margarine.

Mushroom Sauce

Cook 1/2 lb. mushrooms in 4 T. butter or margarine over very low heat for several minutes. Add 4 minced green onions, cook several more minutes. Blend in 2 T. flour, 1 cup water and 1 t. instant chicken bouillon. Add 1/2 cup dry red wine, 1/2 t. sugar and some chopped parsley. Cook until sauce thickens.

Makes about 1-2/3 cups

Mustard Sauce

Add 1 T. prepared mustard to 1 cup of Drawn Butter Sauce. Keep warm.

Old Sour

2 cups fresh lime juice
Bird peppers to taste

1 t. salt

Chop peppers and put in a sterilized bottle along with salt and strained lime juice. Cork tightly and shake well. Let ferment for about 2 weeks at room temperature. This sauce will keep over a year.

Szechwan Sauce

2 cloves garlic, minced
1-1/4 T. minced chili pepper
2 T. soy sauce
2 T. chicken stock

1-1/2 T. sugar or honey
2 or 3 drops sesame oil
1 T. vinegar

Sauté garlic until brown, then add remaining ingredients and heat. Use with shrimp.

Tarragon Honey Mustard

1 cup strong mustard
4 T. honey

3 t. finely chopped fresh tarragon
Tabasco to taste

Mix all ingredients in a blender. Let stand several hours.

Tartare Sauce

Add 1 T. chopped capers, green olives, sweet pickles to one cup mayonnaise. Let stand one hour before using.

Pat Winter's Herb Sauce for Vegetables

Pat Winter, until shortly before her death, ran the House of Herbs in Salisbury, Connecticut. Few people were more knowledgeable about spices, herbs and seasoning than Pat.

3 T. olive oil
1T. butter
1 Medium onion, minced
1clove garlic, minced
2 tomatoes, fresh or canned
1 stalk minced celery

1 T. parsley
1 t. wine vinegar T. butter
1/4 t. rosemary
1/4 t. sugar
Salt and pepper to taste

Heat oil and butter, simmer garlic, onion and celery for 5 minutes. Add cut-up, peeled tomatoes and remaining ingredients. Simmer 10 minutes. Pour over cooked string beans, zucchini, spinach or the like.

Light Batter for Deep Frying

Many people don't like deep fried food because of the heavy batter coating. Here's a light one with fewer calories.

3/4 cup corn starch
1/4 cup flour
1 t. baking powder
1/2 t. salt

1/4 t. pepper
1/2 cup of water
1 egg slightly beaten

Mix first 5 ingredients together. Add water and egg. Stir until smooth.

Beer Batter

Use beer or ale in place of the water in the previous recipe.

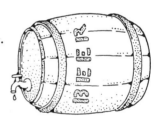

APPETIZERS

Angels on Horseback

Here's an old favorite that's hard to beat!

4 dozen large oysters, shucked
24 slices of bacon
2 cups light batter*
Cooking oil

Lemon wedges
Parsley for garnish
Toothpicks

Cut bacon in half and wrap slice around each oyster. Secure with toothpick. Dip in batter and deep fry in hot oil for about 3 to 4 minutes.
Serve with lemon wedges and garnish.

Makes 38 hors d'oeuvres

* See page 29

Zucchini Appetizer

Here's one from Gail Wien a boating friend who has recently crossed the Atlantic in a 36 foot sailboat.

3 cups zucchini, thin sliced or grated
4 eggs, beaten
1/3 to 1/2 cup oil (not olive)
1/2 t. each: marjoram & season salt or
1/2 cup Parmesan and 1/2 t. Italian season

2 t. garlic salt
Salt and pepper to taste
1 cup Bisquik
1/2 cup grated onion

Mix all above ingredients and bake in a 9 inch x 9 inch pan in water at 350^0 for 30 minutes.

Zippy Cottage Cheese Spread

1 cup cottage cheese
2 t. anchovy paste
2 T. prepared mustard

2 t. minced on
1/2 cup butter, softened
1 T. capers

Omit butter for a low calorie dish.

Mix all ingredients well. Chill and serve on crackers.

Spread #2

1 cup cottage cheese
1 cup cream cheese
1 cup blue cheese, mashed

1 t. Worcestershire sauce
1/2 t. fresh ground pepper

Combine all above ingredients and mix well. Chill.

Eight Dips or Spreads

Mix well, 1 cup cream cheese with 1 cup sour cream. Add any of the following and mix well. Let stand in the refrigerator at least one hour. Add any of the below:

1. One 6 oz- can shrimp, chopped and 1/3 cup chopped green pepper.

2. One 7-1/2 oz. can crab meat, one T. lemon juice and a dash of Tabasco.

3. One small jar of Caviar (red or black) and fresh lime juice to taste.

4. One 6 oz. can minced clams, drained and minced with one t. Worcestershire sauce.

5. One small can deviled ham and 1/2 t. Tiger or Picapeppa Sauce.

6. Three T. Horseradish and one t. grated onion.

7. One small can green chilies, chopped.

8. One avocado, mashed with one t. lime juice, 1/2 t. salt and one small tomato, chopped.

Which ever one you are making, mix all ingredients well and chill for at least an hour before serving. If you plan to use chips, use less cream cheese.

Marlene's Blue Cheese and Egg Dip

I first tasted this dip at a cocktail party at the home of Marlene Wood. A Cajun from Louisiana, Marlene is an excellent cook and you will find several of her Gumbo's further along in this book.

6 hard cooked eggs
1/2 cup sour cream

1/2 cup or 2 oz. blue cheese
2 t. onion salt

Mash eggs and mix all ingredients together. If you have time, let stand in the refrigerator an hour.

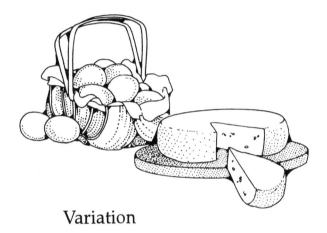

Variation

Add 2 T. fresh dill, chopped fine.

Quick and Easy Paté

8 oz. liverwurst
8 oz. cream cheese
1 t. lemon juice

1 t. steak sauce
1 t. cognac

Combine all ingredients and mix well.

Makes about 2 cups.

Cheese Pot

If you have any cheese that have hardened or dried up ends, the cheese pot is a good way to turn them into a tasty spread. If you don't have old cheese use whatever you have on hand. Cheddar, longhorn, Monterey jack all are good for the pot. With the price of cheese on today's market, a little Velvetta type cheese can be melted in to extend the dish.

1 lb. of whatever cheese you have
2 T. butter softened
3 T. minced onion
Salt and pepper to taste

3/4 t. dry mustard
1 to 3 T. White wine
Dash of Worcestershire Sauce

Grate cheese or run through a food processor or blender. Add remaining ingredients and work out any lumps. Put in small crock and refrigerate before using. The ingredients can be heated to facilitate the mixing.

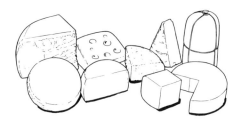

Chicken Wings with Apricot Glaze

2 lb. chicken wings
1/3 cup vegetable oil
3 garlic cloves, minced
2 T. lemon juice

1 t. each: rosemary, thyme and salt
1 bay leaf, crumbled
Pepper to taste
Apricot Glaze*

Cut off wing tips, saving them for stock. In a bowl, mix oil, garlic, lemon juice, herbs, bay leaf and pepper together. Add wings and toss until coated. Let stand in marinade covered at room temperature or refrigerate over night.

Place drained wings on broiler rack and broil for 5 minutes on both sides. Baste generously with Apricot Glaze and broil for 3 minutes on each side or until they are brown.

Serves 4

*Apricot Glaze

1 onion, minced
1 T. butter or margarine
2 T. cider vinegar
1 cup apricot preserves

1 T. soy sauce
2 t. Dijon style mustard
1/4 t. each: ground ginger, cloves,
Salt and pepper to taste

In a small sauce pan cook onion and butter until softened. Add vinegar and reduce. Add apricot preserves, soy sauce, mustard and herbs and cook for about 7 to 10 minutes or until thick. Put glaze through a blender or food processor. Makes about one cup.

Variation

You can have Buffalo Wings by adding 2 or 3 T. of hot sauce to the glaze.

Try Pickapeppa or Tiger Sauce

Avocado Dip

1 large avocado
2 t. lime juice
1 t. grated onion
4 T. mayonnaise

Hot sauce to taste
Salt to taste
Paprika

Cut avocado and scoop out pulp then mash. Mix with remaining ingredients except paprika. Chill. Sprinkle with paprika before serving.

Hot Beef and Cashew Dip, Capt'n Bob

I first tasted this one at a New Year's party in Nassau. Since I have been making it, I have received many compliments.

1 5 oz. jar chipped beef (rinsed and cut in small pieces)
1 cup cashew nuts, crushed or blended
1 16 oz. package cream cheese

Worcestershire Sauce to taste
Cream sherry to taste

Over low heat mix all ingredients until well blended. Add enough sherry to make the consistency of a heavy dip. This should be served in a chafing dish or other warmer and eaten on chips or crackers.

Sugared Nuts

1-1/2 cups sugar
1/2 cup sherry
2 or 3 cups pecan halves *

1/4 t. nutmeg
1/2 t. cinnamon

Boil sugar and sherry until it forms a soft ball when dropped in cool water. Add nuts and spices. Mix until mixture clouds. Cool.

* Most other kinds of nuts may be used.

Diet margarine will keep you slim.

Tuna Paté

1 7 oz. can tuna fish
2 T. grated onion
1/2 cup butter
Pepper to taste
Hot sauce if desired

1/4 t. dry mustard
1 t. Worcestershire sauce
1/4 t. celery seed
Pinch of powdered clove

Mix all ingredients well, put in a small crock or jar and refrigerate over night. Serve on crackers.

Bourbon Dogs

2 lb. franks or Vienna sausage*
1-1/2 cups ketchup
1/2 cup brown sugar
6 oz. bourbon

3 t. grated onion
2 T. prepared mustard
Hot sauce to taste

Cut franks in one inch pieces. Mix all other ingredients in a large enough pot and heat. Add franks and cook 8 to 10 minutes. Let stand about an hour and reheat before serving.

Serves about 15-20 people

* If you can find the little inch long franks they should be used.

Variation

Kilbassa or smoked sausage can be exchanged for the hot dogs.

Spicy Olives

Drain a can of pitted black olives. Place in a glass jar and cover with Worcestershire sauce and one teaspoon of dill weed. Marinate several days in refrigerator. Drain and serve. Save sauce as it can be used again.

Bahama Tim's Italian Fondue

This recipe comes from a boating friend who cruises the Bahamas alone. He picked up this recipe from one of his ex-wives.

1 jar spaghetti sauce
1 loaf of French bread
6 oz. or more mozzarella cheese (or Swiss or Monterey Jack)

Heat spaghetti sauce in sauce pan and cut cheese in small chunks and add to sauce. Stir until melted. Dip French bread in sauce and enjoy!

Dottie's Cocktail Meatballs

2 lb. Hamburger
1 Lb. Pork Sausage(mild)
3/4 cup bread crumbs(seasoned)
3 eggs
2 onions minced
2 T. spicy mustard
2 T. horseradish
1 t. Pickapeppa Sauce
1 t. Worcestershire Sauce
1/2 t. tarragon

1/2 t. basil
1/2 t. thyme
1/2 t. oregano
1/4 t. red pepper
3 T. ketchup
Seasoned salt & pepper to taste
Cream Sherry to taste
2 cans Campbell's Beef Consommé
1-1/4 cups Cream Sherry

Mix first 13 ingredients together in large mixing bowl. Shape into small meatballs and brown in oven on cookie sheet at 350⁰ for about 8 to 12 minutes.

Mix beef consommé and Cream Sherry together in large saucepan and heat until simmering. Add meatballs to sauce and let stand overnight in refrigerator. Re-heat and serve in chafing dish.

Hot Crab Dip

3 8 oz. packages cream cheese
3 7 oz. cans crab meat
1/4 t. garlic salt
1/2 cup mayonnaise
1/2 t. ground dill weed

3 t. prepared mustard
1/4 cup white wine
1 T. minced onion
Salt and pepper to taste
1 dash Tabasco sauce

In top of chafing dish, over boiling water, melt cheese. Add remaining ingredients and serve with chips or crackers.

Variations

1. One cup of sliced almonds and horseradish can be added.

2. This can be baked in 375⁰ oven for 15 minutes instead.

This will serve a mob.

Mexican Chili-cheese

1 lb. Monterey Jack cheese
2 T. minced onions
1 4 oz. can green chilies, chopped

1 lb. can tomatoes,
chopped and well drained

Combine all ingredients in sauce pan and cook over low heat until cheese melts.
Serve hot with tortilla or taco chips.

Pate of Wild Duck or Wild Goose

Boil game bird in salted water with a couple of chopped onions, a bay leaf and one t. of thyme until the meat comes off the bones easily.

Grind meat in food chopper and cream in some mayonnaise, grated onion and a little cognac. Season to taste with mustard, Worcestershire Sauce or what have you. Store in crocks in the refrigerator or put in the freezer for unexpected guests.

Bagna Caudo

This is a fresh vegetable dip that my brother Bill served in his restaurant, "The Pearly Gates Saloon", every Friday night. It was a big hit. You will need a warmer to keep the oil hot.

1/2 cup olive oil
6 cloves garlic, minced

1 small can anchovy fillets
Fresh vegetables

Put oil in sauce pan and add garlic. Cook over very low heat for 15 minutes. Add minced anchovies and stir until smooth. Keep hot over warmer.

Prepare raw fresh vegetables such as broccoli, cauliflower, pepper strips, cucumbers, celery or what have you. Dip vegetables in hot sauce with fondue forks.

Marinated Shrimp

1 lb. shrimp
1/4 cup white wine
2 T. rice vinegar
1 t. celery seed
1 t. dill seed

1 T. minced onion
1/4 cup salad oil
2 T. capers
Salt to taste
Hot sauce to taste

Boil shrimp about 3 minutes and clean. Make a marinade of the above ingredients and cover shrimp. Let stand overnight. May be kept in the refrigerator for a week.

Homemade Pickled Eggs - Canadian Style

Some love 'em and some don't. If you love 'em they are great to have around for a snack or for sundowners. The following recipe makes one gallon and they'll keep for months.

36 hard cooked eggs, shelled
5 cups white vinegar
2 T. salt
4 T. sugar
4 T. lemon juice
1 t. dill seed

1 t. red pepper
2 T. pickling spice
6 slices of fresh lemon
1 t. celery seed
1-1/2(approx.) cups of water

Boil brine 8 minutes. Cool. Place eggs in gallon glass jug or crock. Pour brine over eggs and let sit at least one week before eating. Keep eggs below brine with small plate.

Chicken Livers with Mushrooms

1 lb. button mushrooms
1 lb. chicken livers
3 T. butter or margarine
Soy sauce to taste

Pepper to taste
1/2 cup dry vermouth
3 T. chopped parsley

Clean livers and cut in serving size pieces. Brown livers and mushrooms in butter. Add soy sauce, pepper, vermouth and parsley. Simmer about 10 minutes. Serve warm.

Shrimp Dip

12 oz. cream cheese
1 can cream of shrimp soup
1 can minced clams, drained

1 T. horseradish
1 t. Worcestershire Sauce

Mix all ingredients and chill about one hour before serving.

Shrimp on Toast

Here is a delicious Chinese treat to start your meal or serve at your next cocktail party.

1 or 3 strips of bacon
1 lb. raw shrimp
5 water chestnuts, minced
1 t. dry sherry

1/4 t. MSG
1 t. salt
10 slices day old white bread
Cooking oil for deep frying

Grind bacon with shrimp into paste. Mix with water chestnuts, sherry, MSG and salt. Set aside. Cut crusts from bread and spread on shrimp mixture. Dip your knife in cold water to ease spreading. Cut bread into triangles, 4 per slice.

Heat oil to 350 degrees and fry, shrimp side down, until edges are brown. Then turn and brown on the other side. Drain on paper towels and serve hot.

Cream Cheese and Shrimp

1 can shrimp, small
1 block of cream cheese

1/2 bottle cocktail sauce

Put block of cream cheese on serving plate and drain shrimp and mix with cocktail sauce. Pour over cheese and serve.

Cream Cheese with Chutney

The same as above but pour a jar of Major Grey's Chutney over cream cheese.

Deep Fried Eggplant

We have one of those little electric deep fryers and think it's great for hors d'oeuvres when guests drop in. Egg rolls, fried won tons, shrimp and many vegetables can be served this way.

1 egg plant
Light batter (see page 33)

Hot oil

Heat oil. Peel and cut egg plant into finger sized strips. Dip in batter then fry until golden brown.

Grouper Fingers

A favorite method of cooking fish in the Bahamas and other islands in the Caribbean. This recipe can be done with almost any large white fish fillet such as: snapper, dolphin, skate, shark, snook and etc.
    Cut the fish into finger size pieces and marinate in lime juice for one half hour. Dry well then proceed as above. Serve with tartar sauce.

Variation

Fish fingers can be marinated in lemon juice and a little hot sauce before frying. Dry thoroughly before putting in hot fat. Don't over cook.!

Stuffed Mushrooms - Many Ways

With the advent of the micro wave, stuffed mushrooms are easy and fast.

Wash and pat dry the mushrooms, remove stems and chop. Stuff caps with any of the stuffings and broil in a 400⁰ oven for 6-12 minutes or in a micro wave from 1 to 3 minutes, depending on the ovens.

Stuffings

1. *Sausage:* Sauté bulk sausage with garlic, chopped onion, minced green pepper. Remove from flame, add one beaten egg and some bread crumbs. Mix well then stuff mushrooms. Add grated cheese to top and broil.

2. *Cream Cheese and Dill:* Soften a block of cream cheese. Add mayonnaise, mustard, minced onions or chives and lots of snipped dill or dried dill. Stuff mushrooms and cook until cheese is bubbling.

Variation

Use Gorgonzola or blue cheese.

3. *Paté:* Sauté some chicken livers with chopped mushroom stems, shallots, onions or what have you. Put in a little heavy cream or sour cream, add some cognac and grated nutmeg. Puree the mixture and stuff the mushrooms and broil.

4. *Cheese:* Stuff mushrooms with grated Monterey Jack cheese and top with pimentos or pickles and broil.

Variation

Top with anchovy paste.

5. *Caviar:* Mix some fish eggs with softened butter or margarine. Stuff mushrooms and broil.

6. *Leftovers:* Grind chicken, turkey, pork or any meat hanging around in the refrigerator and mix it with vegetables, add a little mustard or hot sauce or salad dressing or what have you.

Rita's Salsa Dip

1 can refried beans
2 chopped onions
1 jar picante sauce (salsa)
1 can Cajun style stewed tomatoes

8 oz. avocado (guacamole) dip
1 8 oz. pkg. shredded cheddar cheese
1 16 oz. sour cream
Top with shredded cheese

In a 7 x 11 pan, place the above ingredients in layers. Heat in 350 oven or microwave until cheese melts. Serve with your favorite corn chips.

Make two batches, one mild and one hot so that all of your friends will be happy.

Soups & Stews

Cheddar Soup with Ale

2/3 cups shredded carrots
1/4 cup chopped onions
1/4 cup butter or margarine
1/4 cup flour

2 cups sharp cheddar cheese, shredded
2/3 cup ale
Salt and pepper to taste
1/4 t. ground caraway seed

Cook carrots and onions in butter until soft. Blend in flour. Slowly add cheese then beer and seasonings. Heat to simmer. Add more ale if needed. It should be the consistency of a thick pea soup.

Navy Bean Soup

3 cups navy beans
3 qt. water
1 ham bone, hock or one 16 oz. can of
Spam or smoked luncheon meat, cubed
3 large onions, chopped
2 cups chopped celery

3 carrots, thinly sliced
2 bay leaves
1/2 cup (instant) mashed potatoes
1/2 t. thyme
Salt and pepper to taste
1 clove of garlic, minced

Cover beans with water and bring to a boil for three minutes. Remove from heat and let stand one hour.

Put all ingredients, except the potatoes, with the beans in a pressure cooker and cook at 15 pounds pressure for 20 minutes.* Let stand for 5 minutes. Remove cover and return to heat and thicken with potatoes if desired.

4 to 6 servings

* If you don't use a pressure cooker, it will take about two hours to cook the beans. Check water level often.

Easy Substitute

Use canned bean soup with finely chopped luncheon meat, franks or bacon bits, garlic powder and 1/4 cup of minced onion.

Variations

1. Any other dried beans, peas, lentils etc. may be substituted for the navy beans.
2. Add a little sherry wine just before serving.

Easy Broccoli Soup

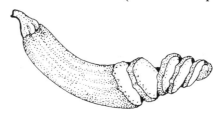

1 bunch broccoli
6 cups chicken broth
1 small onion, minced

4 T. Flour
4 T. butter or margarine

    Chop broccoli and cook in broth with onion until tender. Cool and run soup through a blender or food processor or chop very fine.

    Make a roux with flour and butter over low heat and slowly add soup.

4 to 6 servings

Zucchini Soup

Use same recipe as above but replace broccoli with two pounds of chopped zucchini.

Variations

1. Both may be served chilled
2. 1/2 cup of sour cream may be added with sliced lemon floating on top.
3. Curry powder to taste for a far eastern treat.
4. Frozen broccoli may be substituted for the fresh. (two ten ounce packages for six cups.)

Avocado Soup No. 1

Here is a real easy soup that is a simplification of one from the island of Madeira.

2 cans cream of chicken soup
3 T. minced onion
1 t. chili powder
2 soup cans of water or milk

1 t. grated lemon peel
10 T. minced avocado
Black pepper to taste

Cook all ingredients slowly 6 to 10 minutes stirring often until avocado is soft. Serve with French bread and a fruit salad for lunch.

4 servings

Avocado Soup No. 2

A cold soup that will go great on a hot summer day.

2 large ripe avocados
1 T. onion, chopped
1-1/2 cups chicken broth
1 cup sour cream

1 cup light cream
1 T. lime juice
Salt and white pepper to taste
1/4 t. powdered ginger

Blend all ingredients until smooth. Chill, cover for 2 to 3 hours before serving.

Yield about 4 cups

Bahamian Fish Chowder

In the Bahamas, this soup is made with grouper or snapper. We have used other similar species with good results. The Islander's make a very similar soup with the fish heads which has a wonderful flavor. The heads are removed before the soup is served.

2 lb. grouper or other white fish	1 can evaporated milk
1 lb. potatoes	2 T. butter or margarine
1/4 lb. onions, chopped	1/4 t. thyme or to taste
3/4 cup salt pork, cubed	Hot pepper or Tabasco, optional

Boil fish in salted water to cover until done. Remove fish and cool. Remove bones. Peel and cube potatoes and cook in the same water. Fry pork, thyme and onions in separate pan until light brown. Put in original pot with fish and potatoes. Heat to simmer, remove from heat, add milk and butter before serving.

6 to 8 servings

Shrimp, Clam or Oyster Bisque

1 quart of shrimp, clams or oysters, shelled	2 stalks celery, minced
1 quart half and half	1 onion, chopped
1 pint of milk	Parsley
1/8 lb. butter or margarine	Salt and pepper
1-1/2 t. Worcestershire sauce	Milk crackers, optional

Sauté seafood and onion in the butter several minutes. If you have a blender blend seafood and celery and onion.

Put all above ingredients in double boiler and cook for 30 minutes. Add milk crackers for thicker bisque.

4 to 6 servings

Variations

1. White wine can be added.
2. Rice added early in the cooking can be used to thicken soup.
3. If you don't have half and half use evaporated milk. I have used powdered milk extra thick with good results.

Lobster Carcass Stew

The Florida, Bahamian, or South African lobster tail is the only part of that crustacean that is eaten. The tail is broken from the main body and saved and the rest is chucked back in the water.

This has always bothered me and I have devised the following method of using, all of the lobster and getting another meal from them.

4 to 6 lobster bodies	Rice
2 medium onions, chopped	Sherry
2 stalks celery, chopped	Salt, pepper and thyme to taste
1 green pepper, chopped	

The more heads the better. Boil lobster with onions, celery and pepper about an hour. Remove carcasses, cool, break up and remove all meat. Return meat to pot, add seasonings to taste and reduce liquid by 1/4 (one to two hours). Estimate liquid and add one cup of raw rice to every 4 cups of liquid. Cook 25 minutes, correct seasoning, add sherry and serve.

Variation

Crabs may be substituted for the lobster carcasses.

Calliloo

This stew, invented by slaves, has been upgraded to include rock lobster and shrimp. Every calliloo is different and can be made to your own liking.

2 lb. rock lobster	1/2 lb. eggplant, cubed
2 lb. shrimp	1/2 lb. winter squash, peeled and cubed
1/4 lb. bacon	3 T. peanut butter
1 chicken, cut in serving pieces	1 cup boiled peanuts, shelled
1/2 lb. okra	Seasoning to taste
1/2 lb. onions, chopped	

Fry out bacon and remove from pan.* Add lobster and shrimp and cook until red. Remove. Brown chicken for 15 minutes. Add onions and cook 5 minutes longer. Put all ingredients in a large pot and cover with water and cook until all is tender. Correct seasoning and serve with hot rice.
* Use a Dutch oven if you have one.   10 to 12 servings.

Shrimp Gumbo

Reprinted from my recipe in *Georgia Fishing World*. This recipe has also appeared in *Cruising World Magazine* and the book *People and Food*.

3-1/2 cups canned tomatoes	4 strips bacon
2 cups tomato juice	4 T. flour
4 cups water	2 Large onions, chopped
10 bay leaves	2 cloves garlic, minced
Salt and pepper to taste	3 cups cooked shelled shrimp
3 to 4 T. Worcestershire sauce	1 T. gumbo file
1 lb. fresh okra, sliced	4 cups hot boiled rice

This is four star!

Combine tomatoes, juice, water and seasonings in a large kettle. In a fry pan, fry bacon until crisp, add flour, onion and garlic and cook until brown. Add to large kettle and then add shrimp and okra. Simmer for 1-1/2 hours. Add file and serve on mounds of hot rice in deep soup dishes.

8 to 10 servings

Here's a gourmet meal for you dieters.

Chioppino Shipboard Style

This fish chowder is a West Coast version of Bouillabaisse.

1 green pepper	2 cups water
2 stalks celery	1 pint burgundy wine
4 cloves of garlic	1 small lobster if available
2 cans tomatoes	2 dozen clams in shells
Salt and pepper	1 lb. each: shrimp, snapper, bass and
Olive oil	cod (or any type of fish you have)

Cover bottom of pan with plenty of olive oil. Chop fine pepper, celery and garlic. Fry until just brown. Add tomatoes, wine and water and simmer about an hour. Add fish filleted and lobster chopped in bite size pieces (left in shell). Cook ten minutes. Add shrimp and clams and cook ten minutes or until done. Season to taste.

Variations

1. Several crabs may be added.
2. For seasonings basil, rosemary, marjoram oregano and thyme may be used.

Turkey Soup

After everyone has all they want from the turkey, take the carcass and break it up in to a large soup pot and cover it with water. Add chopped onions, celery, carrots and chicken bouillon. Cook several hours covered until meat falls from the bones. Cool and pick out all bones and run the whole mess through the blender. Return to pot, heat and add one cup of long grain rice for every five cups of soup and cook half an hour. Correct seasoning and add a little sherry and serve hot with corn muffins.

Variations

1.   Add a small can of tomato paste.
2.   Add 1/4 t. saffron.
3.   Add a little hot sauce.
4.   Noodles can be used in place of rice. Shorten cooking time.
5.   If you don't want to use the blender just return meat to pot after bones are removed and thicken with flour in the last few minutes of cooking if desired.
6.   Thyme, rosemary, tarragon or dill may be added.

Kentucky Burgoo

This hearty soup is traditionally served at the Kentucky Derby. There are as many different recipes as there are cooks, so don't feel bad if you don't have all the ingredients, just improvise.

1 gallon salted water
1 lb. of lean beef
1 lb. of lean veal
1 lb. of lean pork
1 lb. of lean lamb
1 lb. of lean chicken
1 cup diced potatoes
1 cup diced carrots

1 cup diced celery
1 cup corn
1 cup lima beans
1 large can plum tomatoes
2 green peppers, chopped
Worcestershire sauce
Salt and pepper to taste

Cube meat and add to boiling water. Simmer until meat is tender. Add vegetables and simmer until the soup is thick. Season heavily with Worcestershire sauce and serve with crusty French bread.

12 to 14 servings

Variations

1. Add gumbo file- for seasoning
2. Season with thyme, basil or bouquet garni
3. Use chicken or beef bouillon to salt water.

Dog Watch Curry Soup

This is a great soup for a fast warm up when your fingers and toes are cold.

Olive oil
2 lb. hamburger or stew beef
2 large onions, chopped
2 grated carrots
2 grated apples

Lemon juice to taste
2 T. flour
1 T. hot curry powder
2 quarts water
Salt and pepper to taste

Fry onions, meat, carrots and apples in oil for about 15 minutes. Sprinkle in flour and curry powder. Fry several more minutes and add water. Cook 15 minutes. Add lemon juice and serve.

4 to 6 servings

Summer Strawberry Soup

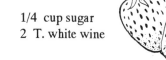

1 16 oz. package frozen strawberries, thawed
1 cup sour cream
1 cup half and half

1/4 cup sugar
2 T. white wine

Blend strawberries. Add remaining ingredients and blend well. Chill several hours or overnight.

4 servings

Variations

1.   Substitute 1 pint fresh strawberries for frozen.
2.   Substitute two 10 oz. packages frozen strawberries in syrup (omit sugar).
3.   Raspberries, red or black, me be used in place of strawberries.

Indonesian Peanut Butter Soup

This is a very easy one to make with items that will usually be on hand.

2 oz. butter or margarine
2 oz. flour
8 cups chicken stock (bouillon)

12 oz. peanut butter
Pepper to taste
Hot sauce to taste (optional)

Melt butter in sauce pan stir in flour, cook several minutes. Slowly add four cups chicken stock and bring to simmer. Blend remaining stock with peanut butter and add to soup. Add pepper and simmer about 10 minutes.

Variations

1.   Add chopped cooked chicken or tuna before servings.
2.   Garnish with a slice of lemon or lime.

Madras curry powder will make it spicy hot!

Senegalese Soup

4 cups chicken stock
4 eggs yolks
2 cups cream
1 cup cooked chopped chicken

1 rind of lemon, grated
1 t. curry powder
Salt and pepper to taste
Worcestershire sauce to taste

In the top of a double boiler heat stock to scalding. Mix separately the egg yolks, curry, salt and pepper, Worcestershire and cream with a blender or whisk. Slowly stir in 1/2 cup hot stock. Then add mixture to remaining stock and cook until thick. Stir all the while. Cool in refrigerator.. Before serving, add lemon peel and chicken and serve cold.

4 to 6 servings

Variations

1. Sour cream may be used in place of cream.

2. Cooked ham or turkey may replace chicken.

3. Egg beaters may be used in place of egg yolks to cut cholesterol.

SALADS

Zucchini Salad

2 small zucchini
1/2 pint cherry tomatoes, quartered
1/4 cup olive oil
1/4 cup vinegar
Salt and pepper to taste

1 t. sugar
1 T. French style mustard
1 clove garlic
1/4 cup fresh basil or 2 T. dry

Cut zucchini in small julienne strips or coarsely grate with a food processor. Put in a bowl with tomatoes. Mix dressing, using a blender if you have one. Pour over zucchini and chill one hour before serving.

2 to 4 servings

Variation

Sliced cucumbers can be added to above.

Reduce calories by using Lo-Cal Dressings on any of these salads.

Pepper and Tomato Salad

1 clove garlic
1 head of lettuce, cut
2 red peppers, cut in rings
4 large tomatoes, wedged
1 large onion, sliced in rings
12 black olives

Dressing:
4 anchovy fillets, mashed
1 T. spicy mustard
2 T. malt vinegar
4 T. olive oil
Salt and pepper to taste

Rub garlic around salad bowl. Line bowl with lettuce. Put in other ingredients. Mix dressing and pour over salad, mix well.

6 servings

Variations

1. Croutons may be added just before servings.
2. Crumbled crispy bacon can be used as garnish.

Fresh Mushrooms Salad

1 lb. fresh mushrooms
1/2 cup lemon juice
3 T. vinegar
1 t. ground dill seed or weed

1 T. tarragon
1/2 cup olive oil
1/2 t. sugar
Salt and pepper to taste

Slice mushrooms thinly lengthwise and put in a bowl. Put in remaining ingredients and chill.

4 servings

Variation

Store bought Caesar or Dijon dressings can be used.

Turkey Coleslaw Salad

4 cups shredded cabbage
1 cup cubed chopped turkey or chicken
1 cup cherry tomatoes, halved

1/2 cup black olives, sliced
Salt and pepper to taste
Thousand Island or French dressing

Combine all ingredients and chill before serving.

Variations

1. Tuna can be used in place of the turkey.
2. Other vegetables may be added. Green or red peppers, onions, chives, green beans or peas.
3. Use anchovy or sour cream dressing.

Off-Shore Salad

This recipe of mine fist appeared in New England Offshore Magazine. I have seen it copied elsewhere in several other magazines. It can be made without fresh vegetables just by opening cans!

1 16 oz. can of tiny peas	2 T. vinegar (preferably rice vinegar)
1 small can sliced mushrooms	1 t. sugar
1 medium onion, chopped	Herbs and spices to taste
3 T. mayonnaise	

Make dressing from mayonnaise, vinegar and sugar in a large bowl. Add drained peas, mushrooms and onion. Spices can be added such as ground dill, tarragon, paprika, celery salt, garlic powder, curry powder or whatever.

Chill or let stand one hour before serving. Can be served on a bed of lettuce.

Serves 4

Potato Salad

Potato salads can be made in many different ways, hot or cold, aspic, loafs, etc.

Rather than give you a recipe, I will list ingredients and you can add as many or mix or match as you like. Let your salad stand in the refrigerator several hours before serving to let the flavors "marry".

To cubed cold cooked potatoes add some of the below:

hard cooked eggs	radishes	celery seed	Russian dressing
minced onion	pickles	sugar	Sweet and sour dressing
green pepper	bacon	mayonnaise	sour cream
cooked peas	pimento	parsley	French dressing
diced celery	cold meat (slivered)	vinegar	milk
cubed cucumbers	salt and pepper	dry mustard	

Many Pasta Salads

Cook 3 cups (8 oz.) pasta according to package directions. Drain. Rinse with cold water to cool quickly and drain well. In large bowl, combine cooled cooked pasta, meat and vegetables. Add dressing and toss lightly. Chill.

6 servings

Select any combination of ingredients from each column to create your own pasta salad:

Cubed or sliced cooked meat
(2 to 3 cups)

chicken
turkey
beef
ham
tuna
salami
pepperoni
crab
shrimp
egg

Chopped or sliced raw vegetables
(1 to 2 cups)

carrots
celery
broccoli
tomatoes
onion
green pepper
zucchini
avocado
radishes
mushrooms
cucumber
cauliflower

Salad dressing
(1 cup)

creamy cucumber
blue cheese
Italian
creamy buttermilk
thousand island
French
creamy Italian
vinegar and oil
Russian
sweet and sour
avocado
hot bacon

Coleslaw with Caraway

4 cups shredded cabbage
1/2 cup mayonnaise
2 T. grated onion
3 T. lemon juice

1 t. caraway seed, crushed
2 t. sugar
Salt and pepper to taste
Paprika

Mix mayonnaise, onion, lemon juice, caraway, sugar, salt and pepper. mix cabbage with dressing and let stand one hour in refrigerator. Re-mix and add paprika to garnish.

6 servings

Cucumbers with Lime

2 large cucumbers
Salt

5 to 6 t. lime juice

Peel and thinly slice cukes. Sprinkle with salt and stir. Let drain for 20 minutes or so. Add lime juice and toss.

4 servings

Variation

Sprinkle cucumbers with ground dill seed or weed.

Spinach Salad

1/2 lb. raw spinach, chopped
2 hard cooked eggs, sliced
1/4 lb. sliced raw mushrooms

1 large onion sliced in rings
Salt and pepper to taste
Salad dressing*

Mix all ingredients except eggs and add salad dressing of your choice or sweet and sour dressing. Add eggs for garnish.

*Spinach Salad Dressing:

1/4 cup wine vinegar
1/4 cup lemon juice
1/2 cup oil

4 T. Parmesan cheese
1/2 t. sugar
Salt and pepper to taste

Chick Pea Salad

The beauty of this salad is that it can be made without fresh greens.

1 can chick peas
1 can sardines
2 hard boiled eggs

2 t. lemon juice
Seasoned salt to taste

Chop eggs and sardines, drain chick peas and mix well with lemon juice.

Hot Potato Salad

This recipe works well in an electric fry pan.

12 medium potatoes
4 hard boiled eggs, diced
1/2 lb. bacon
1/2 cup diced onion

2 eggs, beaten
3/4 cup vinegar
Salt and pepper to taste
Lettuce for garnish

Cook potatoes in jackets, drain, peel and slice while hot. Add eggs. Fry bacon and onion until brown. Drain and save bacon fat. Mix onion and bacon with potatoes.

Add bacon fat to eggs, well beaten. Add vinegar and salt and pour over potatoes. Mix well and heat in electric fry pan on low heat. Serve hot, garnished with hard cooked eggs.

12 servings

Variation

1. Add 1/2 cup chopped parsley
2. One to two T. sugar can be added for sweet and sour.

Kraut Salad

This one comes from Cindy Battle of Tailisman II out of Kingston, Canada. It is a favorite with boaters as it will keep for weeks without refrigeration. Keep it in the refrigerator and add a little kraut to your sandwich.

1 32 oz. sauerkraut, well drained
3/4 cup finely chopped onion
3/4 cup green pepper

3/4 cup celery
1 cup vinegar
1/2 cup sugar

Bring vinegar and sugar to a boil. Add remaining ingredients. Pack in jars, cool and keep in the refrigerator.

Salad Dressings

Sea Island Sweet and Sour Dressing

Here is a different dressing for lettuce or fruit type salads. A real pleasant change!

1/4 cup sugar or equivalent in artificial sweetener
1/4 cup vinegar
1/2 t. salt
1/2 t. dry mustard

Pepper to taste
1 small onion, grated
1/2 cup oil
1 t. poppy seed
1 t. basil or tarragon

Mix all the above together, shake well and chill.

6 to 8 servings

Basic Dressing

1 cup olive or salad oil
1/3 cup vinegar
1 t. salt

1 clove garlic, mashed
1 t. onion, grated
Pepper to taste

Combine all ingredients and shake well.

About 1—1/3 cups

Variations

Dill dressing: Add 3/4 t. crushed dill weed to basic dressing.
Curry dressing: Add 1/4 t. curry powder and 2 T. chutney to basic dressing.
Fine herbs: Add I t. of chopped basil and tarragon to basic dressing.
Tomato French dressing: Add 1/2 t. dry mustard, 1 t. paprika, 1/2 cup ketchup,
1/2 to 1 T. lemon juice and 2 or 3 T. sugar
Low calorie dressing. Use 1/4 cup of oil instead of 1 cup in the above recipe.
Cheese dressing: Add 3 or 4 T. crumbled Roquefort, Blue cheese, Stilton, or other cheeses to the
        above.
Caper dressing: Add 2 T. capers to basic dressing.
Anchovy: Add 1 t. anchovy paste to basic dressing.

Anchovy Salad Dressing

1/2 cup sour cream

1/4 cup mayonnaise

2 T. vinegar

1 T. lemon juice

2 t. anchovy paste*

2 T. parsley

1/2 cup chopped green
onions(scallions, chives, etc.)

Mix all ingredients and chill.

* If you don't have the paste, mash 2 fillets.

Sour Cream Dressing

1 cup sour cream

1 t. dill seed, crushed

2 T. tarragon vinegar

2• t. olive oil

Garlic powder to taste

Salt and pepper to taste

1 t. chopped onion

Blend all ingredients and chill.

Makes 1-1/2 cups

Variations

1. Omit garlic powder and add chopped fruit for aspics.
2. Add 1 T. lemon juice and 3 T. grated horseradish.
3. Add I cup sieved avocado and 1 t. prepared mustard.

FISH & SEAFOOD

Fish

Most of these recipes can be used with various species of fish. You can use this first recipe with any white fillet. But I believe if you have fish such as Grouper, Red Snapper, Cobia, Pompano, etc. that are fresh, it is best to just broil or bake them with a little lemon juice and butter. Don't overcook fish. One of my favorite meals when dining out used to be broiled Swordfish but I have had so many dried overcooked chunks of shoe-leather that I don't order it anymore.

Fish Fillet Parmesan

2 lb. fish fillets	1 T. grated onion
1 cup sour cream*	Salt and pepper to taste
1/4 cup Parmesan cheese	Paprika
1 T. lemon juice	Parsley for garnish

Place skinned, boned fillets in a single layer in a heavily buttered baking dish. Mix remaining ingredients except paprika and parsley and spread over fish. Add paprika and bake at 350⁰ for approximately 25 to 30 minutes. Fish is done when if flakes easily.

6 servings

Variations

Thinly sliced tomatoes can be placed on the fish in the last 4 minutes of broiling.

* One cup of mayonnaise may be used instead of sour cream.

Fish Fillet, Crumbed

2 lb. skinned fillets	3 T. cooking oil
1/2 cup French dressing	Paprika
1-1/2 cups crushed cheese crackers	Lemon wedges

Cut fish in serving size pieces. Dip fish in dressing and roll in crumbs. Place on well-greased cookie sheet. Sprinkle oil over fillets and add paprika. Bake in hot oven (500⁰) for 10 to 12 minutes. Serve with lemon wedges.

6 servings.

Variations

1. Use above recipe but substitute barbecue sauce for French dressing and barbecued potato chips for cheese crackers.
2. Fish Fillets Florentine: Cook fillets on a bed of cooked spinach dotted with butter.

Snapper Corsican

This recipe can be used with most any white fish fillet.

4 snapper fillets	1/2 cup olive oil
1 T. vinegar	12 black olives, chopped fine
2 T. lemon juice	1/4 cup walnuts or pecans, crushed
2 cloves garlic, minced	1 T. dried parsley

Put all ingredients except fish in a jar and shake well. Let sit for one hour. Lightly salt and pepper fillets and brush on sauce. Broil until fish is flaky, add remaining sauce and return to broiler for one minute. Serve with noodles or rice.

Serves 4

Baked Shark with Mushrooms and Cheese

The best tasting sharks are dog fish, mako, hammerhead, lemon, bonehead, sharp nose and blacktip. Freshly caught, shark should be soaked in ice water in which 1/2 tablespoon lemon juice per pound of fish has been added. Refrigerate and let soak about 4 hours. Cider vinegar or double the amount of the lemon juice can be used.

1 to 2 lb. of shark fillets	1/4 cup dry white wine
Salt and pepper to taste	1 cup slivered cheddar cheese
1 cup sliced mushrooms	Fresh parsley for garnish
1/2 cup condensed cream of mushroom soup	

Place skinned fillets in a well greased baking pan. Sprinkle with salt and pepper. Mix mushrooms, soup and wine. Spread over the fish and sprinkle with cheese. Cover and bake at 350⁰ for 20 to 25 minutes or until flaky.

4 servings

Variation

Also great with just lemon better.

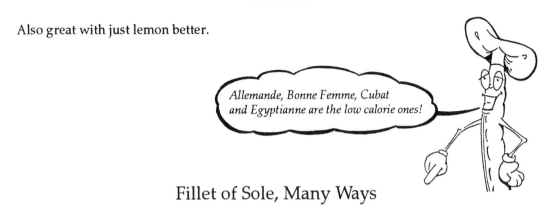

*Allemande, Bonne Femme, Cubat
and Egyptianne are the low calorie ones!*

Fillet of Sole, Many Ways

The sole lends itself to more variations of cooking than any other fish. Whether you use the Dover Sole or any of the flounders, these recipes can be used, to list only a few.

Allemande - Pan fry. Splash with slivered almonds lightly browned in butter.

Bonne Femme - Poached, covered with white wine sauce, garnished with mushrooms and fine herbs.

Chamberin - Poached whole in wine stock then jellied.

Cubat - Poached in sherry wine sauce and mushrooms. Sprinkle with grated cheese and glaze.

Egyptianne - Poached in court bouillon covered with white wine sauce. Placed on fried eggplant slices and garnished with mushrooms and parsley.

Florentine - Poach in court bouillon. Place on lightly cooked spinach leaves and cover with a cheese sauce.

Mornay - Poach in white wine and cover with Mornay sauce.

Nicoise - Pan fry in half butter and half olive oil. Garnish with tomatoes, tarragon, black olives and capers.

Veronique - Poach in white wine, cover with white wine sauce made from Sauterne and heavy cream. Garnish with white seedless grapes.

Trout Florentine

6 trout, cleaned
Salt and pepper to taste
Flour
2 cups cooked spinach
6 slices bacon, cooked crisp

2 cups cooked rice
4 T. Butter
1 t. lemon juice
1 T. parsley, chopped

Combine spinach, crumbled bacon and rice and mix well. Salt and pepper fish and dredge in flour. Stuff fish with spinach mixture and bake in a hot oven until done. Melt butter, add lemon juice and parsley, cook until brown. Pour over fish and serve.

3 to 6 servings

Variation

Instead of butter, use Sherry.

Slivered almonds can be sprinkled over trout before serving.

Blue Trout

This is a favorite way to cook trout in France and Switzerland. It deserves more popularity in this country.

In order for the trout to turn blue it must be freshly caught and not handled much.

Bring to a boil, 1/3 tarragon vinegar and 2/3 water. Kill and gut trout and plunge in the mixture. When the trout turns blue remove from the vinegar solution and place in boiling court bouillon. When the liquid returns to a boil cover pot and remove from heat. Let stand 15 minutes.

1 trout per serving

Broiled Fish with Orange Butter

1 to 2 lbs. fillets*
Salt and pepper to taste
4 T. orange juice concentrate

4 T. butter or margerine, melted
Orange slices
Watercress

* Use skinned fillets of any lean fish such as kingfish, dolphin, snapper,, shark or flounder.
Place fillets in a well greased 2 quart casserole. Sprinkle with salt and pepper. Combine orange juice and butter. Pour 1/2 sauce on fillets and broil 4 to 6 minutes about 4 inches from heat. Turn fish baste and cook 6 to 8 minutes or until done. Garnish with orange slices and watercress.

4 to 5 servings

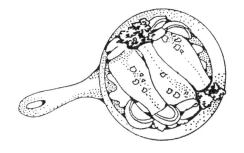

Savory Broiled Fillets

2 lb. fillets
2 T. oil
2 T. soy sauce
2 T. Worcestershire sauce

1 t. paprika
1/2 t. chili powder
1/2 t. garlic powder
Hot pepper sauce to taste

Place fillets, skin side down, on a well greased broiling pan. Mix remaining ingredients and pour over fish and broil about 4 inches from flame for 10 to 15 minutes or until done. Baste twice during cooking with pan juices.

6 servings

Variation

1. This recipe can be baked in the oven or even on top of the stove by following directions mentioned elsewhere in this book. (Use high heat).
2. Open a small can of mushroom stems and pieces and place on fillets before cooking.

Broiled Sesame Catfish

This recipe can be used with most fresh water fish.

6 skinned and dressed catfish	4 T. lemon juice
1/2 cup sesame seeds	1 t. salt
1/2 cup sesame oil	Pepper to taste

Wash and dry fish. Mix remaining ingredients. Dip fish in sauce and broil slowly basting with sauce frequently. Turn and finish about 5 to 7 minutes.

6 servings

Blackened Fish

Blackened fish should be cooked outdoors due to the smoke!

Heat a large cast iron fry pan over an outdoor fire for 10 to 12 minutes. The hotter the better. Dip fillets of grouper, snapper, salmon, redfish, etc. in melted unsalted butter and sprinkle with a mixture of red pepper, thyme, salt and MSG if you like. Place fillets in skillet and top with one T. butter. Cook uncovered 2 to 4 minutes or until charred. Turn, top with butter and cook another 2 to 4 minutes. Serve immediately.

Quick and Easy Cashew Tuna

2 T. butter or margarine	8 oz. cooked noodles
1/2 cup chopped onion	1 can cream of mushroom soup
1 cup chopped celery	2 cans tuna
1 can mushrooms, stems and pieces (drained)	1/2 cup sherry wine
1/2 lb. cashews, chopped	

Sauté onions and celery in butter in a large skillet. Add mushrooms and cook several minutes. Add remaining ingredients. Cook over low heat 15 to 20 minutes stirring occasionally. Add a little water if needed.

4 to 6 servings

Variations

1.   This dish can be baked in an oven. Just mix above ingredients and top with bread crumbs and bake at 325⁰ for 30 to 40 minutes.
2.   Grated cheese can be added. Try 3 ounces of either cheddar or Parmesan. In the stove top method, add cheese just before removing pan from the heat.

Sour Cream Stuffing for Fish

When you are going to bake a fish whole, fill the cavity with the following dressing. Sea bass are good for this dish.

3/4 cup chopped celery	1/2 cup sour cream
1/2 cup chopped onions	1/4 cup chopped lemon
1/4 cup chopped green olives	2 T. grated lemon rind
1/4 cup bacon fat or oil	1 t. paprika
1 quart dry bread crumbs or stuffing mix	1 t. salt or to taste

Cook celery, onion and olives in fat until tender. Combine all ingredients and stuff fish. Any extra stuffing can be wrapped in foil and cooked alongside the fish. Bake in a medium oven until done.

Conch goes good with hot sauce.

Conch, Italian Style

Conch (pronounced conk) comes from the large seashell that you put up to your ear to hear the ocean roar when you were a kid. Almost every home had one as a door stop when I was a lad. It wasn't 'till I made my first trip to the Bahamas that I first tasted conch. I've been hooked ever since.

Conch may be purchased in fish markets in Florida and Eastern New England. Conch should be tenderized by rapping it with a mallet or hammer until the muscles relax. Conch is made into salads, fritters, chowders, deep fried(cracked) and used with pasta sauces.

1 good size conch fillet per person	Tomato sauce
Flour	1 slice Mozzarella cheese
1 or 2 large eggs, beaten	Parmesan cheese
3 T. butter or oil	

Flatten conch between waxed paper or in a zip lock until tender. Dip fillets in flour then egg then flour again. Cook fillets in butter over moderate heat. About 2 minutes per side. Drain.

Place conch in gratin dish or a flat oven proof casserole. Cover with heated tomatoes sauce then cover with mozzarella and sprinkle with Parmesan cheese. Place under broiler for several minutes until cheese is melted and golden.

Shrimp Jambalaya

1 T. oil	1 or 2 cloves garlic, minced
1 T. flour	1 large pepper, chopped
1 lb. diced cooked ham	Salt and pepper to taste
3 cups cooked shrimp	1 t. Worcestershire sauce
2 cups canned tomatoes	4 cups water
2 onions, chopped	1 cup long grained rice
1/2 t. thyme	Pinch of saffron

Brown flour in heated oil. Add ham, tomatoes and shrimp. Add onion, pepper, garlic and spices. Simmer several minutes, add rice and cook over low heat for 20 minutes.

Variations

There are as many variations to this dish as there are Cajun cooks. Jambalaya can be made with chicken, sausage, crabs or crawfish. I have seen Jambalaya recipes with and without saffron.

Serves 6

Shrimp and Crab Quiche

1/2 cup mayonnaise	2 T. flour
1/2 t. salt	1 can crab meat, drained*
2 eggs, beaten	1 can shrimp, drained*
1/4 cup milk	1/4 cup chopped onions
1/2 lb. Swiss cheese, shredded	1 9 inch unbaked pie shell

Heat oven to 350^0 . Combine mayonnaise, salt, eggs and milk. Blend well. Toss cheese with flour and add to mayonnaise mixture then flaked crab meat, shrimp and onions. Mix and pour into pie shell and bake 45 minutes.

* Fresh seafood is better.

Variation

Crumbled bacon can be added.

Shrimp Etoufee

Here is another "Cajun" recipe that will convince you that these people know what they are cooking about.

1 large onion, finely chopped	2 T. flour
3 green onions, chopped	1/2 cup water
3 cloves garlic, minced	1-1/2 cups tomato juice
1/3 cup celery, chopped	1 T. Worcestershire sauce
1/2 cup butter or margarine	Hot sauce or red pepper flakes to taste
1 t. salt	1 lb. cleaned raw shrimp

In a large skillet sauté onions, garlic and celery in the butter until tender. Add flour and cook until light brown. Add water, tomato juice and spices. Simmer uncovered stirring occasionally for 20 to 30 minutes. Add shrimp and cook about 4 to 8 minutes. Correct seasoning and serve over rice.

Serves 4

Variations

1. Use Clamato or V-8 juice instead of tomato juice and add one whole fresh tomato peeled and chopped.
2. This one can still be valid with peppers (chopped) or mushrooms.

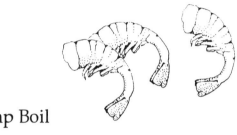

Low Country Shrimp Boil

This dish is as big in the low country around Charleston as the clam bake is in New England. This is an easy dish to prepare and tastes so good, don't pass it by!

I owe this recipe to Capt'n Ralph Vick from Palm Beach Shores, Fl.

2 lb. smoked sausage
2 t. Tabasco sauce
2 lb. fresh mushrooms, whole
2 lb. fresh red potatoes, quartered

6 to 8 ears corn, cut in thirds
2 lb. fresh shrimp, shells on
Salt and pepper to taste

Fill your largest kettle half full of water. Add Tabasco and one tablespoon of salt for every gallon of water. Cut sausage in serving size pieces and add when water starts to boil. Cook five minutes and add potatoes, cook ten minutes, add mushrooms and corn. Cook 10 minutes more. Then add the shrimp. Cover and cook 3 to 5 minutes. Drain.

Serves 6 to 8

NOTE: Frozen mini ears of corn can be used when fresh corn is not in season. Whole canned potatoes can be used, but add them at the same time as the corn. This dish can easily be cooked for large crowds if you have large enough pots! I've cooked this dish for over 50 people and have used 4 or 5 different kinds of sausage such as: kielbassa, southern, Italian, cheese and hot variations.

Use less oil.

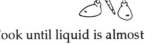

Scampi with Vermouth

2 lb. cleaned shrimp
1/3 cup olive oil
1/2 cup dry vermouth
2 cloves garlic, mashed

Salt and pepper to taste
4 T. chopped parsley
3 T. lemon juice

Brown shrimp in heated oil. Add vermouth, garlic, salt and pepper. Cook until liquid is almost evaporated. Add parsley and lemon juice. Serve hot with rice or noodles.

4 servings

Variation

Add several ounces of slivered almonds halfway through the cooking.

Mussels Marnier

If you have a large cast iron kettle, get it out!

4 servings of mussels
2 cups white wine
1/2 onion, minced
1/4 t. thyme

1 bay leaf
5 T. butter or margarine
Pepper to taste

Scrub, remove beard and soak mussels an hour or so. Bring the wine and other ingredients to a boil for several minutes in a large kettle.

Add mussels and cover pot tightly and cook for about five minutes stirring several times. When done, remove mussels to four wide soup dishes. Let broth sit for several minutes to allow any sand to settle to the bottom of the pot. Spoon juice over mussels and serve.

Variation

One of the most memorable dishes I ever had was the mussels cooked as above and then a morney sauce added to the strained broth and poured over the mussels.

New England Clam Pie

48 soft shell clams, shucked and cleaned
2 cups hot boiled potatoes, sliced 1/4 inch thick
2 onions, chopped fine
5 T. butter or margarine
6 slices bacon fried crisp and crumbled

2 T. flour
Salt and pepper to taste
1/4 cup cream
2 T. parsley, minced
Pastry dough

Fry bacon and set aside. Scrub clams well and steam to open. Reserve liquor. Remove clams. Butter a two quart baking dish. Line bottom and sides with potatoes.

Fry onions and celery in a T. butter until golden. Add clam liquor and simmer until tender. Make a "roux" of flour rubbed with remaining butter and add to clam liquor making a thin gravy. Combine clams, bacon, cream and salt and pepper. Correct seasoning. Pour carefully into casserole, sprinkle with parsley and cover with pastry dough. Prick crust and bake at 450^0 for about 15 minutes or until browned.

NOTE: Remember, don't overcook clams. They get tough if cooked too long. This also applies to all shellfish.

Variation

1/2 pound of sautéed mushrooms can be added just before crust is put on.

Clam Bake

One of my favorite meals is an old fashion New England Clam Bake. Starting out in the morning with raw cherrystones on the half-shell with hot New England clam chowder, hamburgers, hot dogs, cheese and crackers to dull the hunger pangs until the main bake comes on at about 2:00 P.M.

The afternoon fare includes steamed soft shell clams, lobster, corn on the cob, chicken, sweet and white potatoes and watermelon.

Kettle Bake

Clean soft shell clams well and rinse many times until there is no sand or mud in the water. This is very important as sandy clams can ruin a bake.

Put one inch of water in a very large kettle. Put about 20 clams per person in the bottom of the kettle, add potatoes, corn and one lobster per person. Steam for 30 minutes. Cook chicken separately.

Pit Bake

Gather a lot of large stones and stack close together. Build a pit alongside it 18 inches by 2 feet. Build a hot fire on the stones and after the fire has died out roll the hot stones in the pit with a stick. Cover with sea weed about 4 to 6 inches deep. Pile on clams, corn, potatoes, etc. in the pit. Cover with sea weed and cook for 30 minutes or until clams are open and potatoes are done.

Oyster Roast

Along the southeastern coast of the United States the oyster roast is what the clam bake is to the northeast.

An outside fire is prepared and let burn down to a bed of coals. Large sheets of metal such as old signs with the paint burned off are placed on bricks above the fire. The oysters are placed on the metal and covered with burlap bags soaked in water. Then a heavy canvas is put on top. When the oysters are opened they are ready to eat. (Some people don't like them well done, so take them off earlier). Eat them as they are or use a cocktail sauce or the following.

Dipping Sauce for Oysters

1/2 cup tarragon vinegar
1 t. grated onion
2 t. lemon juice
1 t. dill weed

2 t. parsley, chopped
2 t. freshly ground pepper
Salt to taste

Mix well and chill over night.

Broiled Oysters

Open oysters and leave on the half shell placing them in a pan with rock salt or regular salt to hold them level.

1.   Put garlic butter on oysters and broil about 3 or 4 minutes.
2.   Add spinach and a piece of bacon to oyster and broil.
3.   Add lemon juice, parsley and grated cheese and broil.
4.   Add cocktail sauce and a little butter and broil.

Oyster Dressing

Here's another one of my recipes reprinted from Georgia Fishing World. This one appears yearly in the Thanksgiving issue.

2 cups bread, cubes or stuffing mix	2 cups washed oysters
1/4 cup melted butter or margarine	2 T. dried parsley
1/4 - 1/2 t. salt and pepper to taste	1 t. mixed dried herbs (thyme, sage,
Pinch of nutmeg	bay leaf, tarragon)
1/2 lb. sautéed mushrooms	Dry white wine
1/2 onion, chopped	Ginger ale

Melt butter with salt, pepper, nutmeg, onion, parsley and herbs. Add oysters and sear until edges curl. Remove oysters and mince. Mix all ingredients together and moisten with half wine and half ginger ale until desired moistness is reached. Use for turkey, chicken or fish.

Makes 4 3/4 cups

Variation

Onions can be sautéed with the mushrooms.

Crab Sauce Piquante from Marlene Wood

3 doz. crab bodies and claws, cleaned
13 to 15 yellow onions, chopped
8 bell peppers, chopped
5 cups of rotel tomatoes * (cut up)

1-1/2 cups flour
3 cans cream of mushroom soup
2 cans of water
Salt and red pepper to taste

* *NOTE*: If you cannot find this brand, use any kind of canned tomatoes and add red pepper to give it a hot taste.

Cook onions and bell peppers until wilted. Add flour and stir until browned. Add canned tomatoes, soup and water. Cook until well mixed. Season to taste with salt and red pepper.

Throw in crabs and cook for about 10 minutes. Serve over white rice.

Variation

Some people don't like to do any work while eating, so if you prefer you can use crab meat or even copy crab.

You can forget the Tabasco if serving kids and ulcer patients.

Deviled Crabs

1 lb. crab meat
1/2 cup chopped onion
1/4 cup chopped celery
1/4 cup chopped pepper
2 cloves of garlic, mashed
1/3 cup oil
2 cups soft bread crumbs

3 eggs, beaten
Salt and pepper to taste
1 10-1/2 oz. can cream mushroom soup
1/2 t. Worcestershire sauce
1/2 t. dry mustard
1/4 t. Tabasco sauce

Cook onion, celery, pepper and garlic in oil until tender. Combine remaining ingredients and put in crab shells in shallow individual baking dishes. Bake in 375⁰ oven for 15 to 20 minutes.

6 servings

Crab Imperial, Maryland

1/2 cup butter or margarine
2 cups milk
1 t. grated onion
1/2 cup flour
1/2 cup cream
3 egg yolks
1/2 lb. sautéed mushrooms

Salt and pepper to taste
2 oz. dry sherry
1 t. Dijon type mustard
1 lb. crab meat, picked
1 T. Worcestershire sauce
Buttered bread crumbs
Grated Swiss cheese

Melt butter, add onion and flour. Gradually add milk and cream. Stir until smooth. Mix in yolks, mushrooms, salt and pepper. Cook several minutes and add sherry, mustard, crab meat and Worcestershire sauce. Put in a shallow oven proof dish, cover with plenty of cheese and crumbs. Bake at 350^0 until bubbling and brown on top.

6 servings

Variations

1. Use sour cream instead of cream.
2. Add a little more mustard if you like a spicier dish.

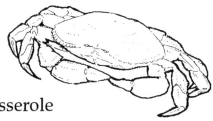

New Jersey Seafood Casserole

To the Crab Imperial, add 1 pound of boiled shrimp, 1 quart poached oysters, 2 cups grated cheddar cheese, the juice of a lemon and 1/2 t. dill weed.

8 to 10 servings

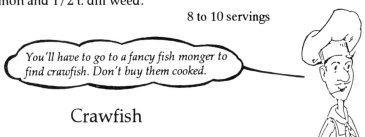

You'll have to go to a fancy fish monger to find crawfish. Don't buy them cooked.

Crawfish

Crawfish, crayfish or craw-dads I do believe is one of my favorite foods. These succulent finger size lobster type crustaceans are mainly harvested in Louisiana (about 20 million pounds!) and very little is exported. That's got to tell you something!

Etoufee of Crawfish

1 lb. crawfish tails
1 cup crawfish fat
1 cup water
2 cloves of garlic, minced
1/2 cup fresh parsley, chopped

2 large onions, chopped
1 cup green onions, chopped
1/4 lb. butter or margarine
Dash of sherry

In a large pot melt the butter. Add the onion and garlic and cook slowly until onions are soft. Add remaining ingredients, cover and simmer for 20 minutes. Serve over hot long grained rice.

2 to 4 servings

Crawfish Steamed Carolina Style

In a large pot put a handful of celery tops and handful of chopped onions. Add a quart of water and a pint of Sauterne wine. Bring liquid to a boil and add a mess of craw-dads and cook 3 to 5 minutes.

Lobster Tails Morney

6 lobster tails
6 T. dry white wine

8 oz. Mornay sauce (see page 21)

Cut underside of tail lengthwise. Broil tails shell side up for five minutes keeping them five inches from the flame. Turn, pour on wine and Morney sauce and broil seven minutes. For large tails add one minute cooking time to each tail.

Serves 6

Variations

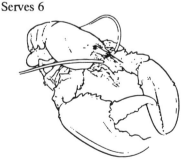

1.   Use lemon butter instead of Morney sauce.
2.   Try Béarnaise sauce.

Seafood Casserole - Gunzinger

For the seafood a mixture of shrimp and fish or crab meat and fish are best but use what you have. The fish should be firm boneless white fish cut in chunks and skinned.

3 cups seafood	1 small can water chestnuts, sliced
2 T. minced onion	1-1/2 cup mushrooms, sliced
6 T. oil, butter or margarine	1/3 cup black olives, sliced
3 cups white sauce	1 cup bread crumbs
1/2 cup dry white wine	1/2 to 3/4 cup grated Parmesan cheese
Salt and pepper to taste	

Sauté seafood in shortening with onion for about 4 or 5 minutes. Add wine and salt and pepper. Add to white sauce. Stir in chestnuts, mushrooms and olives. Pour into a 3 quart greased casserole. Sprinkle in half the cheese and mix. Cover with crumbs and remaining cheese and bake for one hour in 350⁰ oven.

Paella (pie-a-ya)

Here is a favorite from Spain. I have eaten it all over Spain and Portugal and the U.S.A. Every one has been different! The seafood used varies because what is available and what you can afford. The basic ingredients are chicken, sausage (hot), garlic, onions, rice shellfish and saffron.

3 T. olive oil	12 small clams (unopened) scrubbed
1 fryer chicken, cut small	12 or more large shrimp in shells
1 or 2 large onions, chopped	2 lobsters, in shell, cut up
3 cloves garlic, minced	8 oz. cherizo or any hot sausages, sliced
1 T. saffron	8 oz. frozen peas
1-1/2 cups long grain rice	3 large tomatoes, chopped
4-1/4 cups chicken stock	

Heat oil, fry chicken until done. Remove. Fry onion and garlic until soft, add rice, cook gently. Add saffron and stock. Cook about 15 minutes. Add remaining ingredients then cook for about 10 minutes over medium heat, adding more stock if needed.

6 servings

To cut the heat use mild sausage.

Variations

1. Use mussels in place of clams
2. Use crabs in place of lobsters
3. Crayfish, prawns, langoustines, squid, chunked white fish or scallops can be used.
4. This dish may be finished in the oven.

Stir Fry Shrimp with Pea Pods

8 to 10 large shrimp per person
Equal amount of pea pods
1 large onion, chopped
1 clove of garlic, minced
2 strips ginger, fresh
1 can fancy mixed Chinese vegetables

2 stalks celery, chopped
2 to 3 T. sherry
1 T. salt
2 T. cornstarch
4 to 6 T. peanut oil

Mix sherry, salt, ginger and cornstarch with cleaned shrimp and let set at least 30 minutes. Stir fry shrimp in oil in wok or large fry pan. Remove. Do onions, remove. Do pea pods, remove and do other vegetables. Return everything to pan and add a sauce made with 2 T. cornstarch mixed with sherry and soy sauce to taste. Serve with white or fried rice.

Coquille St. Jacques

This is another of my favorite dishes. If you have sea scallops, they should be cut up to the size of bay scallops.

1 lb. scallops
3/4 cup white wine (dry)
6 shallots
3/4 cup Morney sauce
Cracker crumbs

1/2 lb. mushrooms, thinly sliced
Grated Swiss cheese
Parsley for garnish
1/4 cup butter

If scallops are sea scallops, cut in quarters. If bay scallops, leave whole. Put scallops in wine and bring to a boil, then turn off heat and drain, saving liquor.

Slice mushrooms lengthwise and chop shallots. Sauté for several minutes in butter. Remove mushroom mixture from pan and add the wine the scallops were cooked in. Reduce liquid by half and slowly add Morney sauce. When mixture is hot add scallops and mushrooms and fill individual scallop shells or a flat casserole with mixture. Sprinkle with a little of the cheese and crumbs and broil in the oven until brown and bubbling.

NOTE: If you cannot locate shallots use mild onions as replacement.

Shrimp Creole

You can reduce the hot sauce to 1/2 t. and let guests add extra at the table.

1 large onion, chopped
2 cloves garlic, minced
1 T. olive oil
1 green bell pepper, cut into 1/2 inch slices
1 can (15 oz) tomato puree
2 T. Worcestershire sauce
2 t. thyme leaves, crushed

1 bay leaf, crushed
2 t. hot pepper sauce
1 lb. medium to large raw shrimp,
    peeled and deveined
3 t. sugar
Chopped parsley, optional
Hot cooked rice, optional
Freshly ground pepper, optional

Sauté onion and garlic in oil in a 10-inch pan until tender, about 4 minutes. Add green pepper, tomato puree, Worcestershire sauce, thyme, bay leaf and hot pepper sauce. Cover and simmer 5 minutes, stirring frequently. Stir in shrimp. Cover and cook until shrimp are opaque, about 5 minutes. Remove from heat, stir in sugar.

Sprinkle with parsley and serve over rice, if desired.

4 servings, 220 calories per serving

DON'T LOOK AT ME LIKE THAT!
EVERYONE'S RECYCLING
NOWADAYS

CHICKEN DUCK
TURKEY & GAMEBIRDS

Roast Goose with Giblet Dressing and Pear

Very few people in the U.S. ever eat goose (the tame variety). Try one on your next holiday. You'll be pleasantly surprised. Save all of the grease as it is considered a delicacy and is used in place of butter in Europe.

9 to 11 lb. goose
1 bag stuffing mix
1/2 lb. sausage (bulk)
4 oz. raisins
1/2 cup chopped celery

1 onion, chopped
Cooked, chopped giblets
6 pears, halved
Mixed sauterne wine and orange juice
Half and half

Preheat oven to 350^0. Make stuffing by frying out sausage, adding cooked giblets, onions, celery and raisins. Cook until vegetables are soft. Add stuffing and mix well. Add wine and orange juice until it is moist enough. Puncture goose skin all over to allow fat to drain during cooking. Rub with salt and pepper or soy sauce. Stuff.

Roast goose on a rack in a shallow pan for about 20 minutes per pound. About 1/2 hour before goose is done remove one cup of fat from the pan. Put it in an oven proof pan and add the pears that have been coated with lemon juice and then goose grease. Cook along with the goose until tender.

When goose is done pour off fat and save. Carve goose and put on platter with stuffing and pears. Make gravy and serve separately.

About 8 servings

Variations

Use chopped mixed dried fruit in place of or along with the raisins.

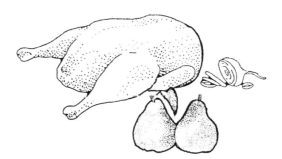

Roast Turkey
(Goose, duck, chicken or pheasant)

The only difference in cooking foul is that with goose and duck excess fat must be removed and moisture retained or added with the others. My mother cooked her turkey in a slack oven with an old dish towel over the bird that was soaked with wine. She also had strips of bacon pinned to the bird. The same moistness can be accomplished by cooking the bird in a bag or foil. A moist dressing also helps somewhat.

Wash and dry turkey and rub with salt and pepper or soy sauce. Stuff bird and cook until meat thermometer reaches 190^0 or leg and thigh move easily. Let cool a few minutes before carving.

Dressings

Oyster dressing	see page 86
Giblet dressing	see below

Cornbread dressing - Use cornbread crumbs and mix with any ingredients below: Cranberry: add fresh cranberries boiled for a few minutes in sugar and lemon juice, added to the water. Use cranberry juice when moistening dressing.

Rice dressing - Use rice in place of crumbs.

Add any or all of the following to your dressing:

Bread crumbs	Sausage	Apples	Oysters	Citron	Pecans
Cornbread	onion	Almonds	Ham	Walnuts	Pineapple
Rice	Mushrooms	Chestnuts	Raisins	Sage	Grapes
Wild rice	Celery	Olives	Prunes	Pickles	Giblets
Mashed potatoes	Salt and pepper	Ginger ale	Wine	Orange juice	

Orange Chicken with Rum

1/4 cup melted butter or margarine
1/4 cup orange juice
1/4 cup rum
1/2 t. orange rind, grated

Salt and pepper to taste
1/4 t. ground ginger
2 garlic cloves, crushed
1 3 lb. fryer, cut up

Preheat oven to 350^0. Mix first seven ingredients and brush chicken parts. Place in shallow baking pan skin side up. Baste 3 or 4 times during cooking. Should be done in one hour. Garnish with orange slices and serve.

4 servings

Variation

Use Cornish game hens in place of chicken.

Chicken Breasts Several Ways

Bone one chicken breast for each person. Skin or leave on as you desire. Flatten slightly with a cleaver or mallet. Fry fillets slowly until tender. Keep warm and serve with any of the following sauces: Horseradish, morney, cream, tomato, hollandaise, mushroom, cheese, béchamel, curry, allemande.

Variations

1. Put a slice of ham on each fillet, cover with sauce and warm in the oven until hot. Garnish.*
2. Put a slice of cheese on the ham and proceed as above.
3. Put chicken breasts on a bed of sautéed mushrooms.
4. Place breasts on a bed of asparagus, broccoli or spinach.
*   Use tomatoes, black or green olives, parsley, pimento, watercress, etc.

Pineapple Chicken with Saffron Rice

1 Large chicken, cut small
5 T. oil
4 T. fresh lime juice
4 T. raisins
4 oz. dark rum
3/4 can tomatoes
3 t. butter or margarine
1 t. soy sauce

1/2 fresh pineapple or 1 can drained, cubed
Soft bread crumbs
1-1/2 cups rice
1/4 t. saffron
1 orange
Salt and pepper to taste
Cornstarch, rum and orange juice

Marinate the chicken parts in lime juice and salt for an hour. Pat dry and fry in heated oil until brown. Reduce heat and cook for 10 minutes more. Add raisins, rum and tomatoes. Mix well and cook until done. Meanwhile, roll pineapple in crumbs and fry in butter until light brown.

Cook rice as directed on package with saffron. Form a nest with rice and put chicken in center. Keep warm. Thicken gravy with a mixture of rum, cornstarch and orange juice or tang and a little sugar. Pour on the sauce and add pineapple and garnish with sliced orange.

4 to 6 servings

Variations

1.   Add hot sauce when cooking chicken.
2.   Use quail in place of chicken.

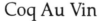

This classic French recipe belongs in every good cook's repertoire.

Coq Au Vin

In France they use this method to tenderize a tough old foul. If you use a fryer, the cooking time may be shortened considerably.

2 T. oil
1 foul, cut up (fryer)
2 t. instant chicken bouillon
1 pint dry red wine
Water
1 lb. button mushrooms

2 Bay leaves
1/2 t. ea. thyme, rosemary and basil
1 can of tomatoes
1 T. sugar
2 doz. pearl onions, whole

A Dutch oven is ideal for this dish. Heat oil and brown chicken, add onions and cook until soft. Add wine and water to cover. Add spices and a little salt if needed, tomatoes and sugar. Cook until chicken is almost done. For a tough old foul, cooking may be from two to three hours. Add pearl onions and mushrooms and cook until done. Correct seasoning and thicken with flour or cornstarch.

6 servings

Chicken, Mexican Style

1 Large fryer, cut up	8 oz. sherry
1/2 cup of olive oil	3 cups chicken broth
4 oz. white corn meal	4 onions, chopped
1/2 cup each: green and black olives,halved	3 to 4 cloves garlic, minced
2 to 3 t. chili powder to taste	1 t. sesame and caraway seed, crushed

Heat oil in large pot. Dredge chicken in corn meal. Brown Chicken slightly and lower heat. Add onions and garlic and cook until onions are soft. Add wine, water and spices. Simmer about one hour. Add olives and chili powder and cook until chicken is well done. Mix corn meal with a little water and add to chicken stirring constantly. Keep adding corn meal until the brew thickens. This dish can be put aside and it will taste much better the following day.

4 servings

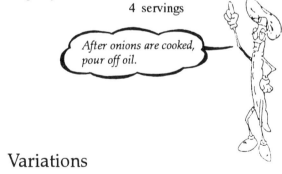

After onions are cooked, pour off oil.

Variations

1. The Northern Italians have a similar dish. Omit chili powder, sherry and caraway. When almost done, add about 1/2 pound of Mozzarella cheese, cubed.
2. Chicken may be taken from the pot and boned before adding the cornmeal.

Chicken Hawaiian

Here is a rich and spicy dish to raise the lowly chicken to a banquet dish.

1 large fryer, cut up
1/4 cup soy sauce
1/2 cup dry white wine
2 T. lime juice
2 cloves garlic, mashed
1 t. curry powder
1 t. candied ginger or powdered ginger to taste
3 onions, sliced

5 T. margarine or butter
Flour (to dredge chicken)
1-1/2 cups uncooked long grain rice
1 can pineapple chunks
1/2 cup toasted slivered almonds
8 prunes, pitted and chopped
1/2 cup port wine

Marinate chicken with soy sauce, wine, lime juice, garlic, curry and ginger for several hours or overnight in the refrigerator. Cook onions in 4 T. butter until golden. Remove from pan and add chicken dredged in flour, then brown. Add onions and marinade and cook 30 minutes covered and 15 minutes uncovered. Cook rice. Brown pineapple in 1 T. butter. Mix rice, pineapple, prunes, almonds and pimentos and heap in the center of a large platter. Place chicken and pineapple around the edge. Add 1/2 cup of wine to drippings in pan and heat and pour over chicken. 4 servings

Variation

Bone chicken after it is done and remove skin. Cut in cubes. Mix all ingredients and stuff in coconut shells.* Make a paste of flour and water and seal tops on shells. Hold upright on a bed of salt and heat at 400^0 for 30 minutes.

* Saw tops off coconut shells with a hacksaw and remove liquid.

Chinese Style Roast Duck

This is Danny Kaye's recipe that I have modified slightly. It's one of my favorites.
One of the main reasons duck is not so popular is that it's greasy. I have found a cure that the Chinese use in their Peking Duck. This process involves putting the duck in front of a fan for 4 to 5 hours. Believe it or not fat or moisture comes out of the duck and the skin dries so it becomes wrinkled and crisp when cooked.

5 pound duckling	3 cups water
3 cups cooked rice	3/4 lb. bulk pork sausage
1 small can crushed pineapple	Anisette
2 small onions, chopped	1 t. anise oil or fennel seed
1 celery stalk, chopped fine	1/2 t. grated orange rind
3 t. instant chicken bouillon	2 T. rice wine vinegar or white
Tang or orange breakfast drink	Cornstarch

Dry duckling as above turning every hour or so. Rub dried duck inside and out with Anisette and let stand. Repeat several times then prick all over. Let stand for two hours.

Fry sausage with anise or fennel seed, onions, celery and pineapple, drained, until brown. Mix in hot rice. Stuff bird and roast in oven for about two hours at 350⁰. Use meat thermometer.

Mix bouillon with water and cook giblets until tender. Remove giblets, mince and return to broth. Add vinegar and enough tang until sauce is sweet and sour. Thicken with cornstarch mixed in cold water until the thickness of heavy cream. Serve separately to use over duck.

4 servings

Spicy Thai Duckling with Three Sauces

My bother, Bill, has also written a cookbook entitled "Burp". Here are a few recipes from his book printed verbatim. Copies available: William Koneazny, 50 Campbell Falls Road, Southfield, MA. 01258.

If you don't know how to steam a full duck, boning it, flattening it with corn starch, then deep-frying the cut up pieces, don't. Just roast the damn thing in a hot oven, nice and crispy, over some chopped celery and onions. In a blender, knock down a seeded green and a red sweet pepper. Throw in 3 cloves of peeled garlic and some fresh coriander or flat parsley. Add 6 seeded (while wearing rubber gloves) fresh jalapeno chilies, 1 tsp. of Thai Fish Paste, 1 Tbs. Thai Curry Paste, 1 Tbs. of Fried Thai shallots, 2 Tbs. sugar, the juice of one lemon, and 1/2 cup of toasted almonds. Grind all well. Fry this mess in oil or pork fat, then add 1 tsp. of corn starch slurried in 1/2 cup of white wine. Add 2 Tbs. of peach marmalade, then wet down the sauce, when thickened, with water or wine until it can pour well over your crisp duckling. Garnish with orange slices and red cherries, and serve on lettuce leaves. Somabitch.

Thut duck gets a two Pedro award!

Chicken Billy Champagne

Marinate a cut-up chicken for 2 hours in a mixture of orange juice, soy, Dash, and squeezed garlic. Fry in a large pan 5 chopped shallots in 2 Tbs. butter, adding 1 chopped, fresh tomato and 1/2 lb. of sliced mushrooms. Add the chicken, and brown a little. Now add 12 blanched pork sausages. Mix 1 cup of Chablis wine with 1/4 cup 7-Up, and pour over chicken in the same pan. Add 3/4 cup of rich chicken broth. Poach at a simmer until the meat is tender, then remove it. Keep Warm. Reduce the stock until delicious, and then add 1/2 lb. more of fresh, sliced mushrooms. Season to taste with salt and pepper. Beat 2 egg yolks with a 1/4 cup of heavy cream and some of the hot pan sauce. Then, with pan fire very low, swirl in the egg yolk mixture.

Cook 2 minutes longer, and, after putting in some butter and a squeezed half lemon, pour over the chicken. Don't you know you've got a plate of chicken that tastes like the best vintage champagne!

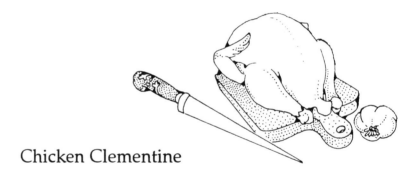

Chicken Clementine

Peel 40 cloves of garlic, bruise them a little. Chop 3 slices of bacon, and fry in a heavy stew pot in 1 Tbs. of butter. Reserve the cracklings to garnish the dish. Add 1 large chopped onion, 1 chopped carrot, thyme, marjoram and the 40 garlic. Backhand in a half cup of fresh basil (or 1 tsp. dried), and then when the vegetables are beginning to brown put in 2 Tbs. of flour, and brown it good. Now add a quart of chicken broth mixed with white wine and 1 oz. brandy. Add a cup of tender-cooked chopped chicken giblets and 1/2 cup of flavored bread crumbs. Meanwhile, oven-brown 2 cut-up fryers in butter, oil and chopped onions. When the chicken is near tender, pour off the fat, put the chicken and gravy in a large casserole, add the strained garlic sauce to the casserole, and cover it up to cook in the oven until the dish is well done. When that cover comes off the dish at the table, all arguments within smelling distance of its waft will crease immediately in supplication. Strangely, there is none of the familiar garlic taste at all.

Doves with Cumberland Sauce

If you are not lucky enough to get some doves, try this recipe with Cornish game hens. Use half a game hen per serving.

12 doves	2 T. Worcestershire sauce
Soy sauce	Cumberland Sauce (see page 24)
3 T. butter or margarine	White wine
2 T. lemon juice	

Split doves in half and rub with soy sauce. Brown in butter. While cooking add lemon juice and Worcestershire sauce. Put doves in a buttered baking dish. Paint a little Cumberland sauce on each and put a little wine in the dish. Cover tightly and bake at 350^0 an hour or more, until done. Remove cover, baste again and serve with Cumberland sauce.

6 servings

NOTE: Cook a mess of rice pilaf and mound it in the center of a large platter. Place doves around the edge and garnish with parsley and white grapes.

Walnut Pheasant in Port and Fruit Juices

Walnuts	White grape juice
1 or 2 pheasants, cut up	Orange juice
Port wine	Salt and pepper to taste
Strong tea	2 T. oil

Put a layer of walnuts in the bottom of a large pot. Cover walnuts with an equal mixture of the wine and tea. Sear birds in hot oil and add to pot. Cover with an equal mixture of orange juice and the grape juice. Cook until tender. Serve with wild rice if you've got a few extra bucks in your wallet. NOTE: This recipe can be used with squab, wild duck or other game birds.

Serves 4 to 6

Variation

Use pecans in place of walnuts.

Mina's Chicken

1 Fryer, cut up
1 can condensed cream of chicken soup
8 oz. sour cream
2 T. oil
1 cup sherry wine

1 onion, chopped
1 can black olives, sliced
1 lb. mushrooms, sliced
Salt and pepper to taste
Cornstarch to thicken

Brown chicken and onions in oil and place in ovenproof casserole. Heat remaining ingredients in pan and when well mixed pour over chicken and put into a 350⁰ oven for 1 to 1-1/4 hours. Thicken gravy with cornstarch mixed with a little water and serve with rice or noodles.

6 servings

Variations

1. Green olives can be used half and half with the black olives. Use less salt.
2. Pour a little warm brandy or rum to the pot after dish is cooked, light and bring to the table flaming.

Far East Barbecue Chicken

3 large cloves garlic, peeled
1 cup unsweetened coconut milk
1 t. grated lemon peel
Salt and pepper to taste
1 t. ground turmeric
1/4 cup fresh coriander leaves

1/2 t. chili paste (optional)
1 3-lb. chicken, cut up
Leaf lettuce
4 T. finely chopped cashews
Lime wedges

In blender grind garlic to a paste, using small amount of coconut milk to smooth mixture. Pour into large bowl. Add remaining coconut milk, lemon peel, salt and pepper, turmeric and chili paste. Skin chicken pieces if desired. Coat chicken well with mixture. Cover tightly and refrigerate. Marinate at least 4 hours or overnight. Prepare barbecue grill and allow coals to become gray. Grill chicken, turning frequently, about 30 minutes or until juices run clear. Serve on platter lined with lettuce leaves. Sprinkle chicken pieces with cashews, coriander and lime wedges.

Serves 4 to 5

Variations

1.   Cut some of the saturated fat by using skim milk and coconut extract in place of coconut milk.
2.   Omit chili paste if you can't stand the heat.

Use of ground Coriander is permitted only if you have tried for the fresh and failed!

Chicken Breasts, Clara Curtis

4 Whole chicken breasts, boned (about 1 lb. each)
1 cup dry white wine
4 T. olive oil
6 shallots or 1 medium onion, chopped
2 pared carrots, sliced into 1/4 inch rounds
1/4 cup Cognac
1/4 cup chopped fresh tarragon or 2 t. dried leaves
1-1/2 T. fresh chopped chervil or 1/2 t. dried leaves

1 t. salt
1/8 t. pepper
1 cup light cream
1 egg yolk
1 T. flour
2 T. butter or margarine
Sprigs of fresh tarragon
1/4 lb. mushrooms, thinly sliced

Skin breasts, cut in half. Heat oil in large pot or Dutch oven. Sauté breasts, several at a time until brown. Remove. Add carrots and shallots, cooking 5 or 6 minutes. Return chicken to pot, heat again, add Cognac, wine, tarragon, chervil and salt and pepper. Bring to a boil. Reduce heat and simmer half an hour. Remove chicken and keep warm. Strain drippings and return to pot.

In another bowl mix cream, egg yolk and flour. Mix well. Stir into drippings, keeping just under a boil. Sauté mushrooms until tender. Pour sauce over chicken and sprinkle with fresh tarragon and the mushrooms.

Serve with rice.

8 servings

This one makes me sweat.

Paprika Chicken

4 T. paprika
1/4 t. cayenne pepper
1 whole fresh long red hot pepper
3 T. corn oil
2 T. butter
2 1 to 3 lb. chickens, cut in to serving pieces

2 medium onions, chopped
3 large cloves garlic, minced
2 T. brandy
3/4 cup chicken stock
1/3 to 1/2 cup sour cream
Salt to taste

Heat the oil and butter in a large heavy stove-top casserole. Brown the chicken pieces over medium-high heat. Remove chicken and set aside. Add the chopped onions to the casserole and sauté the onions. Add the garlic and cook for 1 to 2 minutes. Reduce heat to very low, stir in all the paprika, and cook for an additional minute, stirring constantly. Add brandy; stir to deglaze the pan. Add the browned chicken pieces and mix well. Add the chicken stock and whole hot red pepper. Bring the mixture to a boil over high heat, reduce heat to low, cover, and simmer for 45 to 60 minutes.

Remove the chicken to a serving platter and keep warm. Bring the liquid in the casserole to a boil over high heat, and reduce the liquid by about one-third. Turn the heat to low, and slowly stir in the sour cream, until the sauce is smooth. Add salt to taste. Pour the sauce over the chicken and serve immediately.

6 servings

Serving suggestions: Serve accompanied by egg noodles, plain rice, or boiled potatoes. In Hungary, this dish is traditionally served with small egg dumplings.

LENO, I'M AFRAID WE'LL HAVE TO REGLAZE THIS BIRD.

BEEF PORK
LAMB & GAME

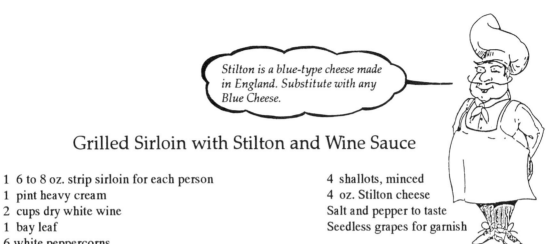

Stilton is a blue-type cheese made in England. Substitute with any Blue Cheese.

Grilled Sirloin with Stilton and Wine Sauce

1 6 to 8 oz. strip sirloin for each person
1 pint heavy cream
2 cups dry white wine
1 bay leaf
6 white peppercorns

4 shallots, minced
4 oz. Stilton cheese
Salt and pepper to taste
Seedless grapes for garnish

Make sauce by boiling together the wine, shallots, peppercorns and bay leaf. Reduce until shallots are just wet. Add cream, bring just to a boil and let simmer 15 to 20 minutes. Whisk in crumbled cheese. Simmer slowly until thickened. Correct seasoning, strain and keep hot. Grill meat over flame. When done pour sauce over, garnish with grapes and serve.

Enough sauce for 6 steaks

Steak Malibu

After you have cooked one side of a sirloin steak, turn over and cross hatch with anchovy fillets like the layout of a tic-tac-toe grid. Put sliced green olives in the squares and broil in the normal way. Don't salt!

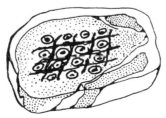

Sauerbraten

3 lb. beef shoulder
1 or 2 cloves garlic
2 t. salt and pepper
2 cups vinegar
2 cups water
1 cup sliced onion

2 bay leaves
1 t. peppercorns
1/4 cup sugar
Fat, flour
1 cup sour cream

Rub meat with garlic and salt and pepper and place in a bowl. Heat vinegar, water, onion, peppercorns and sugar. Pour hot mixture over meat, cover and let stand in a cool place 4 to 8 days, turning meat once each day. Save vinegar. Drain meat. Brown in fat and add 1/2 of the vinegar mixture. Cover pot and simmer 2 to 3 hours until tender adding more liquid as needed. Strain liquid and thicken with 2 T. flour per cup of liquid. Cook until thickened, add sour cream.

6 servings

Variations

Try different flavors of vinegar such as: malt, wine, rice, raspberry, etc.

Roast Beef with Yorkshire Pudding

Have you ever eaten roast beef in a large restaurant and wondered how they get so many medium rare and rare pieces? Their method has the roasts go into a special oven 24 hours in advance. The roast beef oven temperature is about 120^0 (I believe) and the whole roast is cooked rare. People who like well done have their meat popped under a broiler for few minutes.

Recent tests have shown that searing meat before cooking does nothing to seal in juices. Which ever way you cook the roast, I advise a meat thermometer. Remember the meat will cook a little after it's out of the oven, so watch it closely and remove roast before it reaches beef rare, if that is the way you want it.

Cooking time approximately 20 minutes per pound at 350^0.

Cooking time approximately 40 minutes per pound at 250^0.

When roast is done remove from pan. Leave about 1/2 inch of fat in pan and keep it boiling. Beat together: 1 cup of milk and 2 eggs, then sift in 1/4 t. salt and 1 cup of flour. Pour batter in pan and return to the oven. Bake at 450^0 about 30 minutes.

Super Pot Roast

5 to 7 lb. chuck roast	1 can tomato soup
Slivered garlic	1 cup white wine
Sliced black olives	4 large onions, quartered
Soy sauce	4 apples, cored and quartered
3 T. oil	Salt and pepper to taste
Bouquet Garni	Apple juice

Cut slits throughout meat and insert slivers of garlic and olives. Rub meat with soy sauce. Brown in hot oil in Dutch oven. Add soup, wine, spices, salt and pepper. Cover and cook 2 to 3 hours until tender. Add onions and apples and a little apple juice if liquid is needed. Cook another 30 minutes. Serve with mashed potatoes or rice.

10 servings

Variations

1.   One pound of mushrooms can be added in the last 30 minutes.
2.   Use ginger ale instead of wine
3.   Tarragon, basil, bay leaves, oregano can be added to taste.

Roulades

6 slices bacon	1 large onion, chopped
4 individual sirloin steaks, sliced 1/3 inch thick	1 cup water
3 T. spicy mustard	1 can cream of mushroom soup
Garlic powder	1 t. beef bouillon

Fry bacon until crisp. Drain, then crumble. Rub steaks with garlic powder and mustard. Spread chopped onion and bacon evenly over steaks and roll up and secure with tooth picks or skewers.

Brown meat, then add water and bouillon. Cover and simmer until tender (about one hour). Remove from pan, add mushroom soup to pan, heat and serve over roulades. Parsley potatoes and garden fresh peas made a nice accompaniment.

4 servings

New England Boiled Dinner

There are as many recipes for this dish as there are cooks in New England. Cooking this dish on our boat, we use the vegetables we have on hand. Most anything will go. This recipe omits cabbage and turnips which will shock many, but I'm not crazy about cooked cabbage or turnip, so put them in if you like them.

3 lb. corned beef
8 peppercorns
1 clove garlic (optional)
8 large carrots

Cover with water.

8 small onions
8 small potatoes
4 stalks

Put meat in large pot with peppercorns and garlic and cook meat for 2 to 3 hours until tender. Remove meat from pot. Peel and cut up vegetables and cook in the corned beef water until done. Re-heat the meat in the water, drain and serve.

6 to 8 servings

Variations

1. Use daisy ham instead of corned beef.
2. Put a chopped up onion and carrot in water when cooking meat.
3. The following vegetables may be used in place of or in addition to the above: lima beans, broccoli, mushrooms, cabbage, sweet potatoes, winter squash or parsnips.

Scaloppini Al Marsala

A favorite from Northern Italy.

1 lb. lean veal, sliced thin
3 oz. butter or margarine
1/4 cup flour

1 t. salt
4 to 6 oz. Marsala wine

Pound meat thin placing between wax paper and pounding with a mallet or better yet put in a zip lock bag. Mix salt with flour and dip meat slices in mixture.

Melt butter in frying pan and brown meat for several minutes on each side. Add wine and cook several minutes. Serve on warm dish with sauce from the pan.

4 servings

Variation

Scaloppini Neapoli - After browning meat remove from pan and sauté 1 lb. of mushrooms covered about 10 minutes. Return meat to pan, add wine and 1/2 cup of tomato paste and 1/2 cup of cream.

Braised Short Ribs, Aunt Ida

3 lb. short ribs (beef)
1/2 cup flour
2 t. instant beef bouillon
Freshly ground black pepper
3 T. bacon fat or oil

4 onions, chopped
1/2 cup chili sauce
1 small can crushed pineapple
1 t. brown sugar
1 cup water

Dredge ribs in flour and brown in hot fat. Add remaining ingredients. Cover tightly and cook until done. A little water may need to be added from time to time. About 2-1/2 hours cooking time.

4 to 6 servings

Variation

Omit chili sauce, pineapple and water and add 2 cups tomatoes instead. Add water as needed.

Barbecued Spareribs

This is the best barbecued rib recipe I have ever found.

6 lb. spareribs
Boiling salted water
1 onion studded with cloves
1 t. each: rosemary, marjoram, thyme and oregano
2 cloves garlic, minced

1 cup dry red wine
2/3 cup ketchup
3 T. soy sauce
8 t. honey

Cut ribs into serving pieces. Cover with boiling salted water. Add onion and herbs. Simmer until tender (about 50 minutes). Drain and place meat in a shallow pan. Blend all remaining ingredients and pour over meat. Keep in refrigerator until ready to barbecue. Grill over hot charcoal or bake in a 350* oven for 30 to 45 minutes. Baste frequently.

6 to 8 servings

Chalupa

Here's a south of the border recipe from Gayle Weins.

3 lb. pork loin roast
1 lb. pinto beans (cover with water, boil 1 minutes,
cover and let set 1 hour, then drain)
1 t. salt
2 cloves garlic, minced

1 T. ground cumin
1 t. oregano
1 small can green chili
2 T. chili powder

Pressure cook meat 20 to 30 minutes. Add remaining ingredients, cover with water and pressure cook 30 minutes or until bones are easily removed and beans are done. Break up meat and cook without lid until thick. Use as burrito filling by adding:

Grated cheese
Chopped onion
Shredded lettuce
Tomatoes

Avocados
Ripe olives
Hot sauce

Variation

Serve over rice or alone.

Add a little water if needed.

One Pot Sauerkraut Meal

4 T. oil
1 T. caraway seeds
1 lb. of any of the following:
franks, brats, kielbasa, pig
hocks, Spam, ham, pork chops,
spare ribs, etc.
1-1/2 lb. can sauerkraut, drained

1 small onion, chopped
2 cups white wine
1 lb. can potatoes or raw potatoes
cut in quarters
Black pepper to taste
4 to 8 T. honey or syrup

Sauté onion and a little of the meat cut fine and caraway seed until onion is soft but has not changed color. If cooking spareribs or uncooked pork, brown meat then add onions.

Add sauerkraut, honey, wine and meat. Cook 30 minutes over low heat. Add potatoes if raw. Cook 25 to 30 minutes. If using franks, Spam and the like with canned potatoes, cook sauerkraut 25 to 30 minutes, then add meat and potatoes and cook 10 to 15 minutes and serve.

4 to 5 servings

Variation (Hungarian)

Add two T. Hungarian paprika and one cup of tomatoes before adding sauerkraut. When sauerkraut is tender mix 2 T. flour, 1 cup water and 1 cup sour cream. Pour over sauerkraut and cook several minutes. The Hungarians also add cut up green and red peppers.

Ham and Sauerkraut Bake - Armstrong

4 slices ham, cooked

1 can sauerkraut, drained

1 onion, sliced

4 slices Swiss cheese

1 8 oz. can tomato sauce

Put sauerkraut in a low baking dish. Cover with ham slices and then onions. Put a slice of cheese on each ham slice and cover with tomato sauce. Bake in oven for 30 minutes.

Serves 4

Variation

This dish can be prepared in a fry pan using low heat.

Guests will be asking you for the recipe for this one.

Indonesian Pork

2 lb. lean pork, cubed

1 cup peanut butter

2 T. Coriander seed, crushed

2 cloves garlic, crushed

1-1/2 cups chopped onion

2 T. lemon juice

3 T. honey

5 T. soy sauce

1/2 cup chicken bouillon

Pepper or hot sauce to taste

Mix all ingredients except pork in a large saucepan and bring to a boil. Simmer sauce 15 minutes then add cubed pork and cook until done. Serve with white rice. 4 to 6 servings

Without the hot sauce, it's still good.

Variations

1.   I have used this recipe with venison instead of pork and have also used wild pig with much success.

2.   Half of a cup of chopped peanuts can be added to the rice while cooking.

Sweet and Sour Pork

Another of my mothers favorites!

1 lb. lean pork, cut in cubes	2 carrots, sliced
1/2 cup flour	Garlic powder
2 eggs, beaten	1 cup water
8 oz. pineapple	2 to 3 T. vinegar
8 small sweet pickles, quartered	1-1/2 t. sugar
2 green peppers, cut in slices	1 T. molasses or honey
Salt	Cornstarch

Make batter with flour, eggs and salt. Dip pork in batter and fry in hot oil for about 10 minutes. Remove from pan and drain. Put pork in fry pan with pineapple, pickles, pepper, carrots, garlic powder and 1/2 cup water. Cook covered for 10 minutes. Combine remaining ingredients mix with meat mixture and cook for 5 minutes.

Stir-Fry Pork with Linguine

1 lb. boneless pork	1/2 cup milk
6 oz. linguine*	1/4 t. celery seed
2 T. oil	1 t. sesame seed
1 clove garlic, minced	1/3 cup shredded Swiss cheese
1 6 oz. package frozen pea pods	2 4 oz. cans sliced mushrooms
17-1/2 oz. can water chestnuts	

Cut pork into thin strips (1-1/2 x 1/2 x 1/4 inches)/. Cook linguine in boiling salted water until just done. Drain and keep warm. Using a wok or fry pan, heat oil over high heat. Stir-fry garlic 30 seconds. Add pea pods and water chestnuts and stir-fry 2 minutes. Remove from pan and add pork. Cook 4 or 5 minutes and remove from pan. To the wok or fry pan add milk, spices and cheese. When the cheese is melted add vegetables and pork and heat until quite hot. Remove from heat and add linguine and toss.

4 to 5 servings

* You may substitute noodles or other pastas.

Variation

Beef, chicken or shrimp may be used in place of the pork.

American Chop Suey

While any Chinese will tell you that Chop Suey is not a Chinese dish and was invented in the Chinese Embassy in Washington, D.C., this was not a well known fact back in the dark ages when I was a boy, so please excuse the name as I'm sure that the inventor of this dish thought he or she was modifying an oriental recipe.

My mother discovered it in a newspaper and it was a favorite with our family and guests for many years.

2 lb. lean pork, cubed 1/2 inch	1 cup chopped celery
1 cup sliced onions	1 cup rice
1 cup sliced green peppers	1 small bottle green olives, sliced
1 cup sliced mushrooms	

In a large fry pan or wok brown pork well in oil. Remove meat, add onions, peppers, mushrooms, celery and fry until soft. Add more oil if needed. Return meat to pan, add rice and 3 cups of water and cook until rice is done.

Add sliced olives and cook a few more minutes.

NOTE: No salt is needed as the olives will salt the stew.

5 to 6 servings

Variation

Use soy sauce if you don't have any olives.

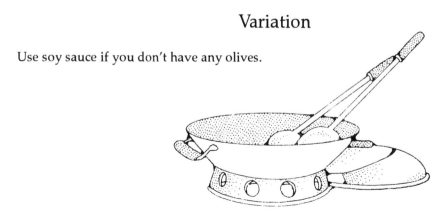

Mushroom Pork

2 lb. boneless pork, 1 inch cubes
3 T. butter or margarine
1 lb. mushrooms, sliced
2 large onions, chopped
Salt and pepper to taste

1/2 t. dried basil
1 t. Hungarian paprika
Garlic powder to taste
1 can cream of mushroom soup
1/4 cup white wine

Brown pork in hot butter. Add mushrooms and onions and cook 5 minutes longer. Add seasonings and cover. Cook at simmer 20 minutes or until meat is tender. Add a little water if necessary. Add soup and wine and cook 5 minutes longer. 6 servings

Variations

1.   Use milk or water in place of wine.
2.   Add several green peppers with the other vegetables.
3.   To make a curry, just add a teaspoon of curry powder and some chopped prunes or raisins.

Shish Kabob

This Mideastern favorite is great on a grill or cooked on a broiler.

2 lb. lean lamb, 2 inch cubes
Marinade
6 firm tomatoes, quartered

6 small onions, halved
12 large mushrooms
3 large peppers, quartered

Marinade

1 t. oregano
Salt and pepper to taste
3/4 cups olive oil

3 T. onion, crushed
1 clove garlic, crushed
3 T. dry red wine

Make marinade and pour over lamb. Let stand 2 or 3 hours, mixing occasionally. Alternate lamb and vegetables on skewers and broil over charcoal or under the broiler. Turning occasionally and brushing frequently with the marinade. Serve with rice pilaf.

4 servings

NOTE: If you don't have skewers make long nests with aluminum foil to hold the shish kabobs and cook under the broiler, turning ingredients once.

Venison Stew

It depends on what the deer has been eating that decided whether you should marinate or not. Deer in many areas eat field corn and they taste like beef with no gamey taste whatsoever, while deer that eat hemlock are very gamey and should be marinated. Of course, marinating also tenderizes, but this can be accomplished by longer cooking. If in doubt cut a piece. If it cuts easily and doesn't have a strong smell, forget the marinade.

6 slices bacon, cut in quarters
3 to 4 lb. venison, cubed, all fat removed
1 lb. onions, chopped
1 lb. pearl onions, whole
1 lb. small mushrooms
6 carrots, sliced
1 cup celery, chopped
1/2 cup ketchup or tomato sauce

2 cloves garlic, crushed
Burgundy wine
Bouillon (beef)
Salt and pepper to taste
Rosemary, basil and marjoram to taste
2 T. sugar
Water

Fry out bacon in a large heavy pot. Add the chopped onions and venison and brown. Add garlic, ketchup, wine and add about as much water as you did wine.

Throw in some instant beef bouillon and the sugar. Add spices. Cover and simmer until meat is tender. Add the vegetables and cook another 15 to 20 minutes.

6 to 8 servings

Venison Schnitzel

Venison makes excellent Schnitzel and is cooked the same way as Wiener Schnitzel. Of course, veal may be used if you have no venison.

4 Venison steaks
4 T. flour
1 egg, beaten
1 cup fresh bread crumbs

Salt and pepper to taste
3 T. oil
Parsley
Lemon slices

Pound the steaks very thin with a mallet or rolling pin. Placing steak inside a zip lock makes the task easier and cleaner. Dip the steak in flour then into the beaten egg and then in the bread crumbs. Salt and pepper and fry quickly in hot oil. One minute per side is usually enough. Garnish with parsley and lemon slices and serve.

Rahmschnitzel

Cook schnitzel as above. Keep hot. Pour 1/2 cup water in pan, add 1 t. chopped capers, 1 t. Dijon type mustard, some paprika and freshly ground black pepper. Bring to a boil and simmer several minutes. Stir in 1/2 cup cream and a few drops of lemon juice. Pour over the schnitzel and serve.

Variation

Sour cream may be used in place of regular cream.

Rabbit with Olives and Polenta

This recipe is from Northern Italy although I have had rabbit cooked this way in Malta served without the Polenta.

4 T. olive oil	1 cup dry white wine
4 to 5 lb. rabbit, cut up	Salt and pepper to taste
4 cloves garlic, minced	2 cups chopped tomatoes
1 t. dried rosemary	1 cup pitted black olives

Brown rabbit in hot oil. Add garlic, rosemary, wine, salt and pepper. Bring to a boil. Add tomatoes and enough water to cover rabbit. Cover pot and simmer for about 1-1/2 hours or until the rabbit is tender. Meanwhile make polenta.

Polenta

6 cups water
2 t. salt
2 cups finely ground cornmeal

Butter or margarine
Grated Parmesan cheese

Bring salted water to a boil. Slowly add cornmeal stirring constantly. Cook over low heat until mixture is smooth and thick. Continue cooking for 20 minutes stirring for 20 minutes. Place polenta on large platter, add butter and cheese. When the rabbit is tender add olives and serve with polenta.

Variation

The olive juice may be used in place of salt when cooking rabbit.
See Sausage with Polenta on page 133.

Hamburger
Sausage Liver

Eggplant Parmesan

Most recipes for this dish call for breading and frying the eggplant. This brings many more calories to the dish, so I tried just using raw slices and it worked fine.

1 lb. hamburger	3/4 lb. Mozzarella cheese
1 small onion, chopped	1 lb. Ricotta cheese
2 large eggplant	Grated Parmesan cheese
1-1/2 lb. tomato sauce	

Brown hamburger and onion and add tomato sauce. Peel and cut eggplant in 1/2 inch slices. Butter a large shallow baking dish. Add a little sauce, then a layer of eggplant, add sauce and thin slices of Mozzarella. Dot with Ricotta, sprinkle with Parmesan, then repeat the process until eggplant is used up or the pan is full. Pour on the balance of the sauce and cover with plenty of Parmesan cheese. Bake in 350⁰ oven from an hour to an hour and one half or until done.

8 to 10 servings

NOTE: You can build this dish in advance and refrigerate or freeze before baking.

HINT: Soak eggplant slices in water with a little lemon juice in it and it will keep the vegetable from turning brown.

Here's one from Paula Armstrong— an Aruba gal.

Marina Cay Casserole

1 lb. ground beef	1 cup red wine
1/2 lb. ground pork	1/2 cup sliced stuffed green olives
4 medium onions, chopped	2 T. capers
1 clove garlic, crushed	1-1/2 t. salt, 1/8 t. pepper
3 T. cooking oil	4 ripe plantains or bananas
1 can (1 lb., 12 oz.) tomatoes	1/3 cup cooking oil
1 6 oz. can tomato paste	4 eggs
1 can (1 lb.) French style green beans	

In a large saucepan fry meat, cook onions and garlic in oil. Add to meat along with next 9 ingredients. Meanwhile, peel plantains, slice lengthwise into 4 strips. Fry in oil until tender and brown. Drain on paper towels. In a 3 quart casserole, layer meat, sauce and plantains alternately. End with meat sauce. Beat eggs and pour over meat. Bake at 350° for 30 minutes.

10 servings

Chili Con Carne

1 lb. hamburger
1 lb. onions, sliced
1 t. beef bouillon
2 or 3 cloves of garlic, minced
1 or 2 one lb. cans kidney beans, drained

1 10 oz. can tomato sauce
Chili powder to taste
1 T. sugar
Red wine
Hot sauce

Sauté hamburger and equal amounts of onions (with spices if added) in large fry pan or pot until hamburger is brown and onions soft.

Drain beans well and add to stew with tomato sauce, chili powder, sugar and wine. Simmer 20 to 30 minutes. Add more chili powder and or hot sauce if wanted. Best when reheated.

3 to 6 servings

Variations

1. Chili originally was made with chunks of beef. Trim fat off stew beef and cook in wine until tender through. Add other ingredients and cook as above.
2. Add 1 T. dried basil, tarragon, thyme, oregano, rosemary, marjoram or one bay leaf.
3. Instead of chili powder, use crushed red pepper and cumin.

Mousaka

This near-eastern dish should be made with lamb, but I prefer beef, so take your choice.

1 large eggplant, peeled
1/4 cup flour
Salt and pepper to taste
1/8 cup of olive oil
1 lb. ground beef or lamb
1 cup chopped onions
1 lb. can tomato sauce

1 small can tomato paste
1 cup white wine
1/2 cup of water
2 cups bread crumbs
1/2 cup grated Parmesan cheese
1/4 cup butter or margarine

Slice eggplant, coat with seasoned flour and fry in hot oil until brown. Drain and keep warm. Brown meat, add onion. Stir in sauce, tomato paste and water. Cook for 15 minutes. Layer eggplant and meat in a 9 x 12 baking pan. Top with cheese, crumbs and butter mixture in a covered dish and bake 40 to 50 minutes at 350⁰. 6 servings

Variations

1. Cube eggplant. Brown meat and onions, add eggplant and cook several minutes. Add sauce and cook until eggplant is tender. Serve with grated cheese at the table.
2. In Greece they line the pan with sliced potatoes, for what reason I don't know. I think it's better without the potatoes.
3. Sprinkle feta cheese throughout the dish.

Shepherd's Pie

For authentic Shepherd's Pie one should use lamb chunks.

There are many recipes for this dish and you can change this recipe as much as you wish and still call it Shepherd's Pie as long as it is covered with mashed potatoes.

3 T. oil	1 t. instant beef bouillon
1 lb. ground beef	1 can peas or string beans
2 Large onions, chopped	3 to 4 cups mashed potatoes
1 can condensed soup*	

Sauté onions and meat and bouillon in frying pan until meat is brown. Remove excess oil then add soup and peas. Stir until well mixed. Put into a greased casserole dish, cover with about on inch of mashed potatoes. Dot with butter and cook in oven at 350° for 45 minutes to one hour. A complete meal when served with salad and garlic bread.

* Cream of mushroom, chicken, tomato, celery, cheddar cheese soup, etc.

Variations

1. Use canned corn instead of peas or beans
2. Use canned lima beans for a vegetable.
3. Put a little garlic powder and/or grated cheese in mashed potatoes.
4. Add mushrooms along with another vegetables.

Sweet and Sour Meatballs

1 3 oz. can chopped mushrooms
1-1/2 lb. hamburger
2 to 3 T. sherry
3 T. minced onions
Soy sauce to taste
1 T. olive oil
1 t. instant bouillon

1 onion, sliced
1 large green pepper, slivered
1 can pineapple chunks
1/4 cup sugar
1/4 cup vinegar
3 T. cornstarch
Hot cooked rice

Drain mushrooms saving liquid. Add water to make one cup. Mix hamburger, mushrooms, sherry, minced onion and 2 t. soy sauce. Shape into balls and brown on all sides in hot oil. Drain off fat. Add mushroom liquid and bouillon. Cook 10 minutes. Add onion, pepper and pineapple chunks. Then sugar, vinegar and cornstarch. Cover and cook 15 minutes. Serve on rice.

4 to 6 servings

Variations

1. They can also be used as an appetizer, served in a warmer.
2. Use chicken, pork, shrimp, lobster, fish or beef chunks for other sweet and sour dishes.

Spicy Meat Balls in Wine Sauce

This is Dottie's specialty.

1 lb. lean pork
1/2 lb. beef round
1 garlic clove
2 small onion
2 parsley sprigs
1/2 t. grated nutmeg
1/4 t. ground cinnamon
1/4 t. ground allspice

1 t. salt
1/4 t. pepper
2 eggs, lightly beaten
3/4 cup dry sherry
3 T. butter or margarine
3/4 cup chicken stock
2 whole cloves
2 T. brown sugar

Grind the pork, beef, garlic, onions and parsley together. Add the nutmeg, cinnamon, allspice, salt, pepper, eggs and 2 T. of the sherry. Mix well. Form the mixture into balls one inch in diameter. Brown the balls on all side in the butter in a large skillet or on a cookie sheet in the oven. Drain the meat balls. Deglaze the pan with the remaining sherry. Add the stock, cloves and brown sugar and bring to a boil. Return the meat balls to the pan, cover and simmer for 10 to 15 minutes, until fully cooked.

5 servings

Hamburg Quiche

1 lb. hamburger
1 cup onions, minced
1 cup mayonnaise
1 cup milk

1 cup grated cheese
4 eggs, beaten
2 T. flour
2 unbaked pie shells

Brown hamburger and onions. Mix well with remaining ingredients. Pour into pie shells and bake at 350⁰ 40 to 45 minutes or until done.

8   servings

Fayaway Meat Loaf

1 lb. hamburger
1 cup onions, chopped
8-10 black olives, chopped
3 T. spicy mustard
1/2 cup ketchup
1/2 t. each of basil, marjoram and tarragon
Tomato and cheese slices

2 eggs, lightly beaten
2 oz. grated cheese
2 T. Worcestershire sauce
2 T. steak sauce
3 T. sherry
Bread crumbs

Mix well all ingredients except crumbs and tomato and cheese slices. Add crumbs until not too moist. Form into loaf in a loaf pan. Place tomato and cheese slices on top and bake in a 350⁰ oven one hour.

6   servings

Variations

1.   Left over vegetables can be added to the mixture.
2.   Four T. of cottage cheese or some sour cream is nice!

Burritos

1 lb. hamburger	1/2 t. sugar
1/3 cup minced onions	2 cups tomato sauce
Salt and pepper	8 flour tortillas
Garlic powder	1 cup refried beans*
Chili Powder	Oil for frying

Brown meat in frying pan. Add onions and seasonings and cook until onions are soft. Add tomato sauce. Cook down until sauce is thick.

Spread 1/8 of refried beans in each tortilla and top with hamburger mixture. Fold in ends and roll up. Start frying in hot oil with flap side down. Cook several minutes on all sides so that they are evenly cooked. Drain and serve hot.

4 servings (2 each)

* If you don't have refried beans, drain a can of kidney beans and fry in oil about 15 minutes.

Variation

Add one heaping T. of grated Monterey Jack cheese to each burrito before folding.

Sour Cream Cabbage Rolls

Here's a low cost dish that originated in Central Europe.

1 small head of cabbage	2 T. spicy mustard
1 lb. of hamburger or ground pork	8 oz. tomato sauce
4 T. minced onion	1 t. dill weed
1 cup cooked rice	1-1/2 cups sour cream
Salt and pepper to taste	Cooked noodles with poppy seed
Garlic powder to taste	

Blanch cabbage in boiling water for 5 minutes. Cool. Remove leaves carefully and cut out course veins. Mix meat and next seven ingredients together. Mixture should not be runny. Place a heaping tablespoon of meat mixture in the center of each leaf. Tuck and roll. Place in a baking dish, cover with sour cream and bake at 350⁰ one hour having the dish covered except for the last 15 minutes.

Serve with buttered poppy seed noodles.

Makes 14 rolls

Chick Peas and Sausage

1 lb. Italian sausage
2 T. butter or margarine
2 large onions, chopped
1 8 oz. can tomato sauce
1/2 t. oregano

1/2 t. basil
1 lb. can chick peas, drained
Salt and pepper to taste
Hot cooked rice

Cut sausage in 1/2 inch slices and brown in butter. Add onion cooking until soft. Add sauce and herbs and peas. Cover and simmer 30 minutes. Correct seasoning and serve on rice.

4 servings

Baked Sausage Apples

8 baking apples
1 lb. bulk pork sausage

1/4 cup bread crumbs
8 large fresh mushrooms

Core apples and arrange in baking dish. Remove stems from mushrooms, put caps aside and mince stems.

Combine sausage meat, crumbs and stems. Fill apples with mixture and cap with mushroom. Bake at 350^0 for 30 minutes.

8 servings

Sausage with Polenta

1 lb. Italian sausage
1 medium onion, chopped
1 clove garlic, minced
1 small can sliced mushrooms
1 cup tomato sauce

1 t. sugar
1 cup canned stewed tomatoes
4 cups hot polenta
Salt and pepper to taste
4 T. grated Parmesan cheese

Cut sausage into serving size pieces and fry until brown. Add the onion and garlic and brown lightly. Add mushrooms, tomatoes and tomato sauce. Cover and simmer about 40 to 50 minutes. Correct seasoning, add sugar.

Meanwhile, make Polenta:

Polenta:

Bring 2-1/2 cups water to a boil with one t. salt. Mix one cup white cornmeal with 1-1/2 cups water, add to boiling water and stir until it comes to a boil. Place over a flame tamer or *very* low heat and cook 45 minutes stirring occasionally. Makes 4 cups. Spread Polenta on a platter and cover with sauce, surround with sausage and sprinkle cheese on top.

4 to 6 servings

Variations

The sausage mixture can, of course, be used over pasta, noodles, mashed potatoes, rice, etc.

Leek and Sausage Pie

Here's a recipe that can be made with a crust, or just cooked in a covered shallow casserole dish.

9 leeks	1/2 cup heavy cream
2 cups chicken broth	1 t. fine herbs*
5 T. butter or margarine	1 T. horseradish
5 T. flour	1 lb. pork sausage links, cooked
Salt and pepper to taste	1 9-inch pie shell (if used)

Just use the white part of the leek. Split down the middle and wash to remove any sand. Cut the leeks into thin strips and simmer in the chicken broth until just tender. Drain and reserve liquor.

Melt butter, blend in the flour and add 2 cups of reserved stock. Simmer over low heat for 10 minutes, add salt and pepper and herbs. Add cream, horseradish and leeks. Correct seasoning and pour into shallow baking dish or pie shell. Arrange sausage links on top of mixture and cover (or add top crust) and bake 20 minutes at 375⁰.

6 servings

* A mixture of tarragon, basil, marjoram, etc.

Variation

If you are unable to find leeks, use mild onions, sliced.

Sausage and Chicken Livers with Noodles

3/4 lb. chicken livers
3/4 lb. sweet sausage
Olive oil
2 cloves garlic, minced
3 tomatoes, chopped

8 oz. red wine
1 T. sugar
1 cup green peas
Cooked noodles

Chop sausage in bite size pieces and cook in oil 10 minutes. Add chicken livers and garlic. Cook 4 or 5 minutes and add tomatoes, sugar and wine. Cover and cook slowly about 45 minutes. Add peas and cook a few more minutes. Combine sauce with an equal amount of noodles.

6 servings

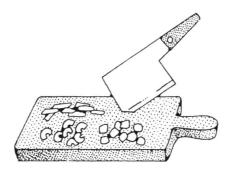

Chicken Livers Casserole

3 to 4 T. butter or margarine
1 lb. chicken livers
1-1/2 cups brown rice, cooked
4 T. white wine
3/4 lb. mushrooms
1 large onion, chopped

2 T. ketchup
1 can cream of mushroom soup
1/3 cup cream
6 oz. almonds, slivered
Salt and pepper to taste

Brown chicken livers in butter, add mushrooms, onions, ketchup, soup, cream and wine. Cook slowly for 20 minutes. Mix with cooked rice in a casserole. Sprinkle almonds on top. Cook in 350° oven for 30 to 35 minutes.

8 servings

Liver with Wine Sauce

2 T. butter or margarine
1 lb. baby beef or calves liver
1/4 cup cream sherry
1/4 cup consommé or beef broth

2 t. chopped parsley
1 t. chervil
1 t. basil
1 T. Cornstarch

The secret of cooking liver is to cook it fast and remove it from the pan just before the last of the pink is gone from the center (cut with a knife to test).

Fry liver in butter. Remove from pan and keep warm. Add remaining ingredients except cornstarch. Cook for 6 to 8 minutes longer. Mix cornstarch with a little water, add to gravy. Stir until thickened and serve over liver.

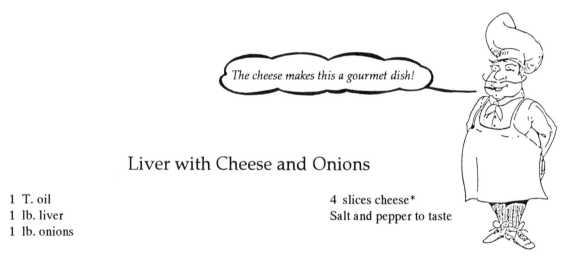

The cheese makes this a gourmet dish!

Liver with Cheese and Onions

1 T. oil
1 lb. liver
1 lb. onions

4 slices cheese*
Salt and pepper to taste

Sauté onions in oil. Remove from pan. Fry liver on one side turn. Cover each of the 4 servings with the onions and top with cheese. Cover and turn heat low until cheese melts.

Serves 4

* Most cheese may be used such as: Swiss, Muenster, Cheddar, Velvetta, etc.

Venison Liver Creole

This dish can be made with any kind of liver if you don't have a deer handy.

1 lb. Venison liver, sliced
1/2 cup flour
1/2 cup vegetable oil
Salt to taste
6 slices bacon
1 cup onions, chopped

1 large green pepper
1 large red pepper
2 ribs celery, chopped
1 large can tomatoes
Seasoned pepper to taste

Cut liver into bite size slices and dredge in the flour and salt. Fry in hot oil until just done (several minutes). Remove liver. Fry bacon until crisp. Remove. Sauté onions, peppers and celery in bacon fat. Drain off excess fat, add tomatoes and simmer about 10 minutes. Crumble bacon and add to pan. Add liver and cook about 3 minutes. Serve over a bed of hot rice.

6 servings

Tamale Pie

This is the Mexican version of the Shepherd's Pie. Instead of mashed potatoes, corn bread is placed over the top of the meat mixture. I first tasted this dish at the home of Olin Howland a movie actor (106 movies). Olin had a home in Northwest Connecticut where he was well known for his culinary ability.

1 lb. hamburger
1 t. instant beef bouillon
1 lb. onions, chopped
3 bell peppers, chopped
1 cup canned corn

1 cup black olives, halved
1 small jar pimentos
Chili powder to taste
1 corn bread mix

Use a cast iron frying pan. Fry out hamburger, onions and peppers. Mix in remaining ingredients.

Use packaged corn bread mix. Follow batter directions. Pour over hamburger mixture and cook in a 375⁰ oven until cornbread is done.

4 to 6 servings

MY TAMALE PIE EVEN MAKES PEDRO PEPPER CRY.

VEGETABLES

Quick Green Beans Gourmet

1 lb. fresh green beans or
1 package frozen green beans or
1 can green beans
3 T. margarine or butter
1 onions, chopped

1 small can of mushrooms, drained
1/2 t. instant bouillon
1 cup sour cream
Paprika

Sauté onions and bouillon in hot butter or margarine. Add mushrooms and cook several minutes. Cook fresh beans until just tender, thaw frozen beans or add canned beans drained. Add sour cream and paprika, heat but do not boil.

Serves 2 to 4

Variations

1. One t. of tarragon can be added when cooking mushrooms
2. One T. fresh dill or 1 t. dried can be used in place of tarragon
3. Use condensed cream of mushroom soup in place of sour cream. Add a little mushroom juice if sauce is too thick.
4. Add chopped water chestnuts to any of the above variations.
5. A can of Chinese noodles can be added just before serving.

Easy Marinated Vegetables

1 can peas
1 can beans, French style
1 onion, sliced
1 cup celery, sliced
1 can corn
3/4 cup salad oil

3/4 cup vinegar
1 T. sugar
3/4 t. dill weed
1 t. tarragon
Seasoned salt and pepper to taste

Combine all ingredients. Marinate in refrigerator 12 hours. Drain and serve cold.

6 to 8 servings

Spiced Green Beans

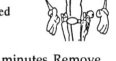

Here's a quickie I invented that really dresses up canned beans.

1 lb. can string beans
2 oz. sherry
1/2 t. dry mustard
1 t. onion bits or flakes

1/2 t. honey
2 t. lemon juice
1 clove garlic, minced

Drain bean liquid into saucepan. Add all ingredients except beans. Simmer 3 or 4 minutes. Remove from heat. Add beans and let marinate for one hour. May be served hot or cold.

2 to 3 servings

Lima Beans with Sour Cream

Canned vegetables are great to have on hand for unexpected company. Lima's come out of the can better than most vegetables and with the addition of sour cream they greatly improve. 1/4 onion, minced 1 lb. canned lima beans, drained 1 T. butter or margarine 2 oz. white wine

Salt and pepper to taste 4 T. sour cream 1 T. ketchup

Melt butter in saucepan, add onion and fry slightly. Add lima's (drained) and warm over low heat. Add wine, salt and pepper, sour cream and ketchup. Heat, but do not boil.

4 servings

Worlds Best Lima's (for a crowd)

3-1/2 lb. dried baby lima's
4 ham hocks, chopped
3 lb. smoked sausage, chopped in 1/2 inch slices
(use several kinds)

3 giant onions, chopped
6 or 7 tomatoes, peeled and chopped
Chicken bouillon to taste

Soak beans overnight, fry meat and onions, add lima's, tomatoes and wine. Cook over low heat for about an hour or more. Add water if more liquid is needed. This dish is better if prepared a day ahead, refrigerated and re-heated.

Serves about 20

Flo Clarke's Beans

2-1/2 onions, chopped and fried in oil
2 cans kidney beans, drained
1 ham bone with lots of meat and fat
1/4 t. celery seed

1/2 t. basil
3 T. tomato paste
2 cups water

Put all ingredients in a pot and cover. Simmer about one hour and 30 minutes. Add more water if needed.

Variations

1. Navy, pinto or most other dried beans can be used.
2. Use a can of stewed tomatoes in place of tomato paste.

Canaan Valley Sporting Club Beans with Bourbon

By using canned beans you can have a dish that compares to slow oven baked beans in a short time.

2 1 lb. cans baked beans
1/4 lb. salt pork or bacon, diced
1 onion, chopped
3 T. mustard

1 cup ketchup
4 T. honey
1/4 cup bourbon

Mix all ingredients except the bourbon and cook over low heat about 30 minutes. Correct seasoning and add about 1/4 cup bourbon or to taste.

8 servings

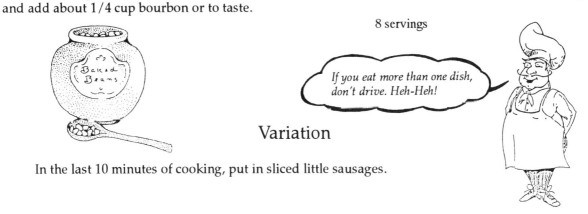

If you eat more than one dish, don't drive. Heh-Heh!

Variation

In the last 10 minutes of cooking, put in sliced little sausages.

Polish Beets

12 small beets or equivalent
2 T. vinegar
2 T. sugar
3 T. olive oil
Salt and pepper to taste

1/2 t. dill seed, ground
1 T. flour
1 T. lemon juice
1/2 cup sour cream

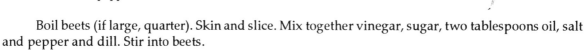

Boil beets (if large, quarter). Skin and slice. Mix together vinegar, sugar, two tablespoons oil, salt and pepper and dill. Stir into beets.

Heat one tablespoon of oil in sauce pan and blend in flour. When smooth add lemon juice and beets. Add sour cream and heat, but do not boil.

About 4 servings

Two great ways to cook broccoli.

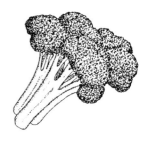

Broccoli Siciliana

1 or 2 bunches of broccoli
8 oz. dry red wine
1 anchovy fillet
Olive oil

Several onions, sliced
1/2 lb. Mozzarella or Monterey Jack
    style cheese

Put wine in blender with anchovy and blend several seconds. Put olive oil in pan and add trimmed, peeled broccoli in small pieces. Cover with onions, then the cheese cut in 1/2 inch cubes. Half fill the pot with the wine and cook until the broccoli is tender. This cooks well in a wok.

4 to 6 servings

Broccoli Casserole - Joy Towne

Here's one that's very rich but it's worth the extra calories every once in a while.

2 10 oz. packages frozen broccoli
1 can cream of mushroom soup
1 cup mayonnaise
2 eggs, beaten

1 chopped onion
1 cup grated sharp cheddar cheese
1/2 cup pecans, chopped

Cook frozen broccoli as per directions. Drain well and add soup and mayonnaise. Mix well, add eggs, pecans and onions. Put in a well greased casserole, sprinkle cheese on top and bake for 30 minutes in 350^0 oven. If this is done on a stove top, cook over a flame tamer on low heat and sprinkle cheese on top when almost done.

6 to 8 servings

Variation

Almonds, slivered or sliced water chestnuts can be added instead of the pecans. To cut out some of the baddies, use egg beaters and low cal mayonnaise.

Carrots, Grand Marnier

1 lb. carrots
1 cup water
2 T. butter or margarine

1/4 t. salt
2 oz. Grand Marnier
1 T sugar

Cut carrots in small strips and add to saucepan with water, salt and sugar. Cook until tender. Drain, add butter to pan and re-heat. Add Grand Marnier and cook several minutes.

4 servings

Variations

1. Cointreau or hazelnut liqueur may be used.
2. Use wine instead of liqueur. Add a little fresh or dried mint with the water when cooking.

Baked Corn and Mushrooms

2 cans corn
4 T. butter or margarine
3 T. flour
2 cups milk
1 cup sharp cheddar cheese, grated
2 eggs, beaten
1 t. sugar

1/2 t. dry mustard
2 onions, chopped
2 small cans mushrooms
1/4 t. tarragon
1 small can pimentos
Salt and pepper
Bread crumbs

Beat eggs lightly. Sauté onions in butter, blend in flour, add milk slowly and add grated cheese. Add seasonings, pimentos and sugar. Stir in corn and eggs. Put in buttered casserole, sprinkle with crumbs and bake at 350⁰ for 35 minutes.

6 servings

Variations

This dish can be done on top of the stove in a double boiler. Leave crumbs off and cook over low heat until set.

Fried Corn

1 can corn, drained
1 to 2 T. oil
Salt and pepper to taste

1 onion, minced
Paprika

Heat oil in fry pan, cook onion until soft, add corn, salt and pepper and cook 10 minutes. Add paprika on top and serve.

2 to 4 servings

Variations

1. Corn and cooked potatoes can be mixed together for home fries.
2. Add 1/4 cup green pepper. When cooked, add one cup of sour cream.
3. Fresh corn, cut from the cob can be used.

Cucumber with Bacon

Here's a different dish that will have your guests asking for the recipe.

3 to 6 medium cucumbers, 1/4 inch slices
1/2 lb. bacon
1 egg beaten
Soft bread crumbs

Salt and pepper to taste
Optional:
      garlic powder, onion powder
      or curry powder

Sprinkle cucumbers with salt and let drain for 30 minutes. Fry bacon over low heat until crisp. Remove and keep warm. Drain cucumbers and pat dry. Dip in egg then crumbs. Fry in bacon fat until golden. Stir in bacon cut in one inch pieces and serve.

4 to 8 servings

Variations

1. The optional spices can be mixed with the egg or crumbs.
2. Use zucchini in place of cucumbers.

How can anything so easy to cook taste so good?

Eggplant Provencial

1 large eggplant, peeled and cut in cubes
3 tomatoes, peeled or canned
1 large onion, minced
2 green peppers, chopped large
1 clove garlic, minced

1 t. sugar
3 T. olive oil
oregano
Salt and pepper to taste

Sauté garlic, onions and peppers in olive oil until limp. Add eggplant, tomatoes and seasoning. Cook over low heat until eggplant is tender.

2 to 4 servings

Variations

1. Add grated parmesan cheese just before servings. Remember the cheese is salty so have dish under salted if you plan to add cheese.
2. Add 1/4 cup chopped black olives while cooking. Omit salt.
3. Add a heaping tablespoon of capers while cooking.
4. Tomato sauce can be used in place of tomatoes.
5. Add several ounces of red wine.

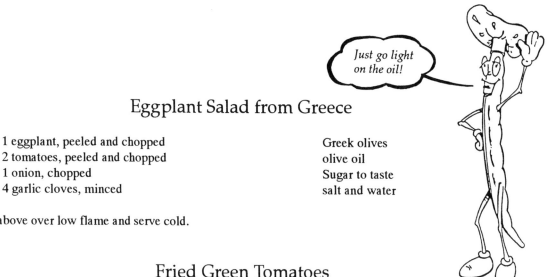

Just go light on the oil!

Eggplant Salad from Greece

1 eggplant, peeled and chopped
2 tomatoes, peeled and chopped
1 onion, chopped
4 garlic cloves, minced

Greek olives
olive oil
Sugar to taste
salt and water

Cook above over low flame and serve cold.

Fried Green Tomatoes

Green Tomatoes
Light batter, see page 29

Salt and pepper to taste

Slice tomatoes and pat dry with paper towel. Dip tomatoes in batter and fry in a hot skillet.

Variation

Tomato slices can be dipped in sugar before batter for a sweeter tomato taste.

Creamed Onions

2 lb. small white onions
1/4 cup butter or margarine
1/4 cup flour
Salt and pepper to taste

1 cup milk
1 cup cream*
1 t. thyme
Nutmeg to taste

Cook onions until tender. Melt butter, blend in flour, salt and pepper. Add milk and cream slowly stirring all the while, add thyme then onions. Heat, then add nutmeg just before serving.
*Omit cream and add more flour. See thick white sauce.

Variations

1. Cook onions in white wine, drain, then add to cream sauce.
2. Use instant beef bouillon in place of the salt.
3. Add 2 T. grated Parmesan cheese to onions just before serving.

Peppers and Onions Mediterranean

5 T. olive oil or salad oil
1 lb. onions, sliced
1 lb. peppers, cut up
1/2 lb. can tomato paste

Beer
Sugar to taste
Salt and pepper to taste

Put all ingredients in large frying pan and moisten with enough beer to keep from burning. Use enough sugar so that mixture is not acidy and a little sweet.
A great sauce to use on grinder-type sandwiches or serve as a vegetable.

Variation

Add a pound of link or Italian sausage and bake above mixture in oven at 350⁰ about one hour.

Microwave Baked Onions

If you like onions you will love them this easy way. Use peeled medium sized onions, one per person. Place in a baking dish. Make a split in the top. Put in a pat of butter or margarine and grate some nutmeg over the top. Cover with plastic wrap and cook for about 3 or 4 minutes per onion. Check book that came with your oven for exact time for number of onions you are cooking.

Variation

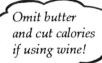

Omit butter and cut calories if using wine!

Put a little dry white wine in bottom of dish before cooking.

Grandma's Potato Pancakes

Potato pancakes are a fast way to use up potatoes. People will eat two to three times as many spuds this way as any other. Served with sausages they are a full meal.

2 lb. potatoes	2 eggs, slightly beaten
1 T. salt	1 T. grated onion
2 T. flour	Oil for frying

Peel and grate potatoes into a bowl. Add remaining ingredients and mix. Heat oil or fat in frying pan. Cook as you would any other pancake. Serve with apple sauce, sour cream, ketchup or butter on the side.

NOTE: The potatoes will darken if left exposed to the air for long. If the batter is to sit any length of time, place some plastic wrap directly on the mixture.

The potatoes may be grated in a food processor or a blender.

Potato pancakes take quite a bit of time to cook, so I always have two pans going at once.

German Raw Fried Potatoes

Here's one that my grandmother used to cook every Saturday night when we would come home from our weekly fishing trip. The meal would generally consist of pan fried fish, sausages, wilted lettuce, German potatoes and fresh biscuits. I can still taste those suppers! Use twice as many potatoes as you would for other potatoes dishes.

Peel 8 to 10 potatoes and slice on a four cornered grater or use a food processor making thin slices. Put 3 to 4 T. bacon fat or oil in a heavy frying pan and cook over medium heat. Don't turn until the potatoes get crusty on the bottom. Cook until done. Salt and pepper to taste.

4 to 5 servings

Swiss Potato Casserole

6 medium red potatoes	1/2 t. nutmeg
2 t. salt	2 cups shredded Gruyere cheese
Pepper to taste	2 T. butter or margarine
1/2 t. basil	3/4 cup chicken broth(hot)
1/2 t. paprika	

Pare and thinly slice potatoes. Place layers of potatoes, cheese and spices in a casserole. Dot with butter and pour broth over all. Bake at 350⁰ about one hour. Add more broth if needed. Top should be brown, broth absorbed and potatoes tender.

4 to 6 servings

Hash Brown Potatoes with Sesame

5 T. butter or margarine	4 baked potatoes, cubed
4 T. minced onion	1/4 cup cream or milk*
2 T. sesame seeds	Salt and pepper to taste

Melt butter in fry pan. Add onions and sesame and cook until lightly colored. Add cubed potatoes, salt and freshly ground black pepper, then cream or milk. Cook until potatoes are golden.

* If you use milk, add a T. of powdered milk to thicken.

Haitian Glazed Sweet Potatoes

6 large sweet potatoes
1 cup port wine

2/3 cup apricot jam
4 T. butter or margarine

Boil potatoes 30 minutes in salted water. Drain, peel and slice. Place in casserole, Combine wine and jam and pour over potatoes. Dot with butter and bake for 1/2 to 3/4 hours at 350⁰ . Baste often

6 to 8 servings

Variations

1. Use peach jam instead of apricot.
2. Use sherry or Chablis instead of port.
3. Add a little nutmeg before cooking.

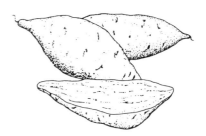

Bavarian Cooked Sauerkraut

2 lb. sauerkraut, drained
4 strips of bacon
1 onion studded with cloves
1 tart apple, chopped

4 to 6 T. sugar or syrup
2 t. caraway seeds
Dry white or ginger ale
Freshly ground pepper

Place the strips of bacon in the bottom of the casserole. Drain the sauerkraut and place in casserole. Add the onion studded with cloves and put in center of casserole. Add chopped apple (leave peel on), sugar, caraway seeds, white wine to cover kraut and freshly ground pepper. If more liquid is needed after half way of cooking, add some beef or chicken stock to barely cover*. Cover casserole and bake in 375° oven for one hour or until stock is absorbed. Serve with pork, ribs or sausages.

6 to 8 servings

* Taste kraut before adding stock so you don't get it to salty. Add ginger ale if stock is to salty. Also, there is now low sodium bouillon on the market which might be better to use here.

Spinach with Sour Cream and Wine

2 lb. spinach
1/4 cup water
2 T. butter or margarine
1/8 t. nutmeg

1/4 cup sour cream
1 small can mushrooms (optional)
2 T. Madeira or cream sherry
Salt and pepper to taste

Cook spinach in water until soft. Squeeze out water and chop fine. Add butter, nutmeg, sour cream, salt and pepper and wine. If using mushrooms sauté for a few minutes before adding. Reheat and serve.

Variations

1. Add grated Parmesan cheese at last moment in reheating. If planning to use cheese, use less salt.
2. Heavy cream can be substituted for sour cream.
3. Can be put in buttered casserole covered with bread crumbs or wheat germ. Add several slices tomato for decoration and heat in oven until hot.
4. Use a cheese sauce in place of sour cream.

Butternut or Acorn Squash in Pressure Cooker

1 large butternut or 3 acorn squash, cut in pieces and seeds removed
1/2 t. garlic powder
Salt and pepper to taste
Margarine or butter

Honey or brown sugar
Nutmeg
White wine

Follow your cooker directions for winter squash except substitute wine for cooking water. Adding garlic powder, salt and pepper and honey (2 or 3 T.) before cooking. Cool, remove from shell, mash with butter and nutmeg. Correct seasoning and reheat if necessary before servings.

4 to 6 servings

Variations

1. Can be baked in oven in baking pan at 350⁰ for about one hour and fifteen minutes. Split in half, score deeply, moisten with wine, butter, garlic and spices and bake until done.
2. Cooked as in basic recipe, but use water in place of wine and moisten with cream when mashing.
3. Use ginger or cinnamon in place of nutmeg.
4. In the microwave oven, this dish can be done 8 to 12 minutes.

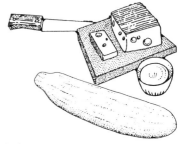

Zucchini Parisian

1 zucchini per serving
Salt and pepper to taste
1 t. tarragon
Butter or Margarine

Cubed cheese:
1 lb. cream cheese
1 lb. Roquefort cheese

This recipe calls for peeling the zucchini. If you can't find squash of serving size carve them so they are. If they are large the seeds should be removed.

Peel zucchini and soak in cold salted water about half an hour. Put tarragon in cooking water and place squash on a rack in a large pot just above the water. Cover and steam. Do not let the squash get to soft. Cream both cheeses together, cut a slit in zucchini and stuff with cheese mixture. Keep split side up (use crumbled foil if needed), brush with butter and broil for 4 or 5 minutes or until cheese is melted.

Variations

1. Most other cheeses can be used.
2. Zucchini can be steamed in chicken broth. Add one t. instant chicken bouillon to one cup of water.
3. Pop them in a broiler or microwave oven until the cheese is melted.

Zucchini Sweet and Sour

Allow six small zucchini for four people

6 small zucchini, sliced	3 T. olive oil or butter
2 T. honey	Salt and pepper to taste
3 to 4 T. vinegar	

Cook in fry pan or heavy pot. Put oil in pan, heat and add zucchini, honey and vinegar. Sauté at medium heat until cooked.

6 to 8 servings

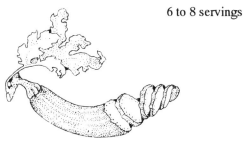

Stuffed Zucchini

The following mixtures can be used to stuff eggplant or large squash.
Cut large zucchini in half lengthwise and scoop out seeds and about half the flesh. Salt and pepper.

Mid-Eastern - Sauté cut up lamb and garlic and onions. Mix with cooked rice. Stuff squash and bake in at 350⁰ oven until squash is tender.

Italian - Mince an anchovy fillet and heat in a pan with 2 T. olive oil and one can of plum tomatoes. Cook 5 minutes and add enough bread crumbs to absorb liquid. Stuff and proceed as above. Note: Chopped olives may be used instead of anchovy.

Mexican - Stuff with chili con carne. Cover with grated Monterey Jack cheese and pop under the broiler for 4 or 5 minutes.

American - Sauté hamburger and onions. Mix with rice and proceed as above.

Broiled Tomatoes

This is a dish we have two or three times a week when the garden tomatoes are coming faster than you want.

Place foil on the broiler tray of your oven. Slice tomatoes 1/2 inch thick and cover the tray with them. Sprinkle with salt, MSG if you use it, pepper, dill, basil, garlic powder and cover with grated Parmesan cheese. Place a dot of butter on each and broil 4 to 5 minutes or until cheese is melted.

Variations

1. This dish can be baked in a hot oven if you don't have a broiler.
2. Other herbs such as tarragon or oregano can be used in place of the basil and dill.
3. Sliced muenster, Monterey Jack, Blue or Swiss cheese can be used in place of Parmesan.
4. Cover with pesto sauce before broiling.
5. Little squares of bacon add a nice flavor.

Omit cheese for lo-cal.

Acorn Squash with Apple Butter

3 Acorn squash (1/2 per person)   3/4 cup of apple butter
3/4 cup butter or margarine   Grated nutmeg to taste

Split squash lengthwise and remove seeds. Boil squash in salted water for 10 minutes and drain cut side down. Arrange squash cut side up in a buttered baking dish. Put 2 T. of butter and 3 T. apple butter in each squash. Bake in 350⁰ oven for 45 minutes or until done. Season with nutmeg.

6 servings

Variations

1. Use honey in place of apple butter.
2. Use cinnamon in place of nutmeg.
3. Can be stuffed with any of the stuffing under stuffed zucchini.

BREAKFASTS

Breakfast Dishes

Of course, any dish may be eaten for breakfast, but in America the standards are bacon and eggs, cereal or toast and coffee. The following are a list of foods that may give you some ideas so that your menus won't get in a rut.

One of my favorites when we have overnight guests is scrambled eggs with mushrooms, link sausages, fried bananas, home fried potatoes, pastry and coffee, an old favorite of my grandmother.

Fruit:

Sliced avocado with lemon juice.
Fresh fruit cocktail. Add a little lime juice to highlight the flavor.
Bananas fried, baked, sliced in orange juice.
Stewed prunes.
Grapefruit, fresh or broiled
Melon, musk, honeydew, cantaloupe, balls, with sherbet.
Strawberries in wine, sugared or with rhubarb.
Apples baked with honey.
Berries, fresh in cream.

Fruit juices:

Apple	Grapefruit	Tomato
Apricot	Orange	V-8
Clamato	Pineapple	
Cranberry	Prune	
Grape	Tangerine	

Others:

Tang
Gatorade

Drinks:

Coffee	Milk
Tea	Buttermilk
Cocoa	Postum

Eggs:

Fried, sunny side up, over light, South American (add 2 T. water to pan and cover until yolks whiten).

Scrambled - add, chopped ham, sausage, bacon, chives onions, mushrooms, peppers, chicken livers, shrimp, lobster, etc. Scrambled eggs are improved by putting a teaspoon of cottage cheese with each 2 eggs. (Thanks, Bob Steele).

Poached - poach in chicken broth. Eggs Benedict - place Canadian bacon on toasted, buttered English muffin, place a poached egg on top and top with hollandaise sauce.

Omelets - asparagus, cheese, chicken, mushroom, lobster, shrimp, kidneys, fried potato, fine herbs, truffles, tomatoes, peppers and onions.

Sweet Omelets - Apricot jam and one T. brandy, 3/4 cup cranberry sauce, jelly or jam or fruit.

Baked or Shirred - In buttered custard cups bake at 350⁰ about 15 minutes. Line cups with sautéed chicken livers, sausages, Roquefort cheese, or other cheeses. Cover with mornay, hollandaise, white mushroom or cheese sauce. May be baked in tomatoes, potatoes, mashed or baked or spinach nests.

Eggnog - 1 cup of milk, 1 egg, sugar, nutmeg and vanilla. Blend all in blender.

Boiled - hard cooked, soft boiled.

Potatoes - Raw fried, home fried (add onions, corn, mushrooms, etc.), French fried (serve in cream sauce), mashed potato cakes, potato pancakes, baked potato skins, sweet potatoes with fruit.

Meat - Any meat may be served with breakfast but the following are more generally presented. Bacon, sliced, Canadian, pork sausage, links or patties, ham steaks, beef steaks, hamburger, chipped beef on toast, liver, chicken livers and kidneys.

Fish - Trout, kippers, pan fish, shad roe, caviar, cat fish, cod fish cakes.

Cereal - Hot, cold, a hundred different varieties.

Pancakes - Add blueberries, chopped peaches, rum, cinnamon, etc., French toast or waffles.

Bread - Rolls, biscuits, English muffins, corn muffins, bran muffins, toast (white, rye, raisin, pumpernickel, French, sourdough, etc.), donuts, croissants, Danish, etc.

Dairy - Milk, buttermilk, cottage cheese, cream, yogurt(fruit flavored), cheeses.

Breakfast sandwiches - Ham or bacon and egg. Canadian bacon and jam on English muffins.

Breakfast vegetables - Beans (baked or refried), cucumbers, tomatoes (sliced, broiled or fried).

Some Different Pancakes

Blender Apple Pancakes:

In container or blender, put 1 cup milk, 1 apple, quartered and cored, 1 egg, 2 T. sugar and 2 t. melted butter. Cover and blend at low speed until apple is chopped. Add 3/4 cup sifted flour and 1 t. baking powder. Mix at high speed until blended. Cook as regular pancakes.

8 to 10 cakes

Rum-Banana Pancakes:

Mix 2-1/2 cups sifted flour, 1/2 t. salt and 1 t. baking soda. Add 2 cups buttermilk, 2 T. oil, 1 egg, 1 t. cinnamon, 2 bananas, sliced and 1 oz. dark rum or rum extract. Mix well and cook in fry pan.

Breakfast Casserole from Phyllis Dodge

2-1/2 cups herb-seasoned croutons
2 cups shredded sharp cheddar cheese
1-1/2 cups sliced mushrooms
2 lb. bulk sausage
1 medium onion, chopped

6 eggs
2-1/2 cups milk
1 10 oz. can cream mushroom soup
3/4 t. dry mustard

Preheat oven 350°F. Grease 8 x 8 inch baking dish. Arrange croutons in single layer. Sprinkle cheese and mushrooms over croutons. Fry sausage and onions, drain on paper towels. Place sausage over cheese. With wire whisk beat in large bowl, eggs, milk, soup and mustard. Bake at 350° until firm throughout (test with straw). May be refrigerated and re-heated.

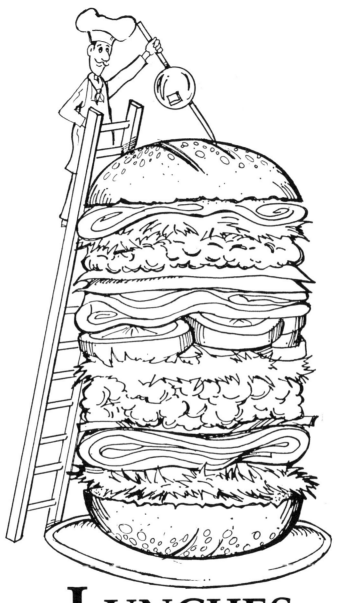

LUNCHES

Some General Rules for Sandwiches

1.   The filling should be as thick as one slice of the bread or 1/3 the sandwich.
2.   The sandwich should be moist, yet firm.
3.   The sandwich should be toasted, if need be, to strengthen the bread.
4.   If you are going to put tomatoes or pickles on a sandwich for a lunch box don't place it near the bread, put lettuce, cold meat or cheese between so the bread doesn't get soggy.
5.   Putting the sandwich in the microwave oven for a minutes melts the cheese and makes it taste better.
6.   Put at least three different ingredients on each sandwich.
7.   Serve olives, pickles, chips, etc. with the sandwich.

Sandwich Ideas

Egg, Cheese and onion - Fry egg on one side, flip and add a slice of American or Swiss cheese and melt. Put mayonnaise on both sides of the bread. Add thinly sliced onions to sandwich. A sandwich that tastes better than you might expect.

Grilled Cheese with Tomato and Bacon - Fry bacon and add with tomato to cheese sandwich. Season with mustard and mayonnaise and butter on outsides of bread. Grill in frying pan until cheese is melted, turning halfway through cooking.

Rubin Grill - Corned beef or Pastrami or even ham on toasted rye bread with a little warm sauerkraut and a slice of Swiss cheese. Use a little mustard on the bread. Close sandwich, butter outsides and grill in fry pan or melt cheese under a broiler.

Tuna and Hard Cooked Egg - Mash 3 hard-boiled eggs with a drained can of tuna, plenty of mayonnaise and t. of grated onion and a bit of horseradish.

Western - Cook chopped onion, pepper and ham in butter or margarine in a heavy skillet about five minutes. Beat eggs with salt, pepper and a little milk or cream. Add to above ingredients and fry as you would an egg sandwich.

Sardine with Tomato - Drain a can of sardines and mash in a bowl with one T. of mayonnaise, 1 t. prepared mustard, 1 t. onion, chopped and Worcestershire sauce to taste. Serve on toasted rye bread with tomato slices and lettuce.

Hot Tuna Bake - Mix one can of drained tuna with 1/4 lb. cubed Swiss cheese, 2 T. minced onion, 4 T. chopped olives, 1/4 cup celery, minced, 1/2 cup mayonnaise and 2 oz. of spicy mustard. Mix all ingredients and spread on English muffins and bake in 425^0 oven until cheese melts.

Ham, Chicken and Cheese - Use a slice each of ham, chicken and cheese of your choice. Add thinly sliced onions and mustard and mayonnaise.

Pork and Sauerkraut - A slice of cold roast pork with sauerkraut and spicy mustard. Put in microwave for 1 minute.

Egg Salad - Boil several eggs, mash with sandwich spread. Add any or all: olives, minced onion, minced celery, chopped pickles, a can of deviled ham, cream cheese or capers.

Liverwurst - On rye bread, build sliced liverwurst, sliced tomato and sliced onion. Use any or all: mayonnaise, mustard or relish on the bread.

Turkey and Dressing - Toast lightly white or rye bread. Spread cranberry sauce on bottom slice, add sliced turkey, stuffing and put mayonnaise on the top slice.

Cornish Pastry (Pasties)

These delicious little pies were first brought to my attention by Dick Brooks on one of our Bahama Cruises.

The Cornish housewife made them for the lunch boxes of their tin miner husbands.

The pie had a savory meat stew in one end and dessert in the other end. He ate one end for his main meal and then ate his dessert from the other end.

Pastry   Fruit pie filling   Meat stew

Make a rich thick beef or chicken stew. Roll out pastry about 9 to 10 inches round. Fill as shown below:

Press to seal between stew and pie. Seal around edge with fork. Brush with beaten egg and bake in a quick oven until golden.

These are still served in pubs throughout England, but they have left out the dessert section. I have had them in Northern Michigan and the filling was hash!

Barbecued Bananas

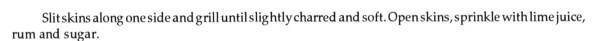

A great accompaniment when grilling steaks or for the beach barbecue.

1 firm banana for each person
Fresh lime juice

Brown sugar
Rum

Slit skins along one side and grill until slightly charred and soft. Open skins, sprinkle with lime juice, rum and sugar.

Variation

The above recipe may be baked in an oven with the skins removed first or cooked in a frying pan.

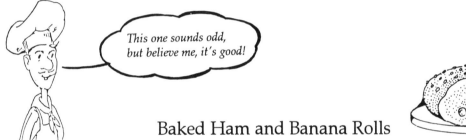

This one sounds odd, but believe me, it's good!

Baked Ham and Banana Rolls

This is a recipe that comes from Trinidad. Everyone likes this dish. A perfect luncheon dish served with a salad.

6 thin slices cooked ham
mustard
6 firm bananas, peeled

1 can cheddar cheese soup*
1/4 cup milk
1/2 t. ground nutmeg

Spread ham slices with mustard and wrap each piece of ham around a banana mustard side in. Place ham banana rolls in a oiled oven proof dish. Make cheese sauce over low heat or heat soup with a little milk. Pour over bananas. Grate nutmeg over top and bake in 425⁰ oven for 10 minutes.

3 to 6 servings

* Make a cheese sauce using cheese whiz or the like.

Spanish Omelet (American Style)

If you go to Spain and order a Spanish Omelet, you will get an omelet with just fried potatoes added.

8 to 10 eggs (2 or 3 eggs per person)
1 chopped green pepper
1/2 onion, sliced thin
1/2 can pimento, chopped
1/2 cup tomato sauce

1/2 t. sugar
Salt and pepper to taste
4 T. butter or margarine
2 T. cottage cheese, milk or sour cream

Sauté pepper and onion in 2 T. butter or margarine. Add drained pimentos and cook several minutes. Add tomato sauce and sugar and cook until sauce thickens slightly.

In a bowl, slightly beat eggs with cheese and salt and pepper. Heat a good fry pan, melt butter and then add eggs. Lift eggs from bottom with a fork so that omelet will set without bottom browning. When omelet is set, add 1/2 of the hot sauce and fold in half, cover with remaining sauce.

4 to 5 servings

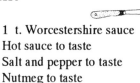

Welsh Rarebit with Rum

1/4 cup milk
1 T. butter or margarine
1 lb. sharp cheddar cheese, grated
1/4 cup dark rum (optional)
1 egg., beaten
1/4 t. dry mustard

1 t. Worcestershire sauce
Hot sauce to taste
Salt and pepper to taste
Nutmeg to taste

Melt butter in top of double boiler*. Add cheese and rum and stir until melted. Add remaining ingredients and serve over toast or biscuits.

6 servings

* I have cooked rarebit in a saucepan without a double boiler by using a flame tamer over very low heat.

Variations

1. Add beer or ale in place of rum.
2. By adding a little tomato sauce or ketchup you have blushing bunny.
3. Add 1 jar shredded dried beef (washed). Omit salt.
4. Add a small can of tuna, shrimp, crab meat or oysters.

Glen's Barbecue Cups

If you are ever speeding in the waters of Chatham County, Georgia you are very likely to be pulled over by the patrol boat. Along with your ticket, you might also get a recipe or two from Glen Deaton, a gourmet cook as well as an enforcer of the law.

Biscuit dough*	Butter or margarine
Parmesan, cheddar and Swiss cheese	Barbecue sauce (see below)

Grease muffin tin with butter. Make small pie shells. Fill with barbecue sauce that is cooked and hot. Top with the cheeses (grated) and place in a 350^0 oven for 10 to 15 minutes until pie shells are done and filling bubbles.

Barbecue Sauce

1 lb. hamburger, browned	1 jar chunky style spaghetti sauce
2 large onions, fried	Barbecue sauce to taste

Cook all together for 10 minutes.

Variations

Use your own barbecue sauce with pork, chicken, etc.
* Bisquick mix or canned dough can be used.

RICE   PASTA
PIZZA & FRITTERS

Rice Cookery

Many people have trouble cooking rice so I will tell you here how you can have perfect rice every time.

Use Uncle Ben's long grain converted rice:

1 cup rice	1 t. lemon juice
2-1/2 cups liquid*	1 T. butter or margarine
1 t. salt	

Bring liquid to rolling boil, add rice, bring back to boil, cover and turn heat to low so liquid is at a slow boil. Cook 18 minutes. Stir several times during last 5 minutes of cooking. Turn off heat and let sit 5 minutes.

* Try cooking rice in 1 cup white wine and 1-1/2 cups water.

Variations

1. One cup of tomato juice and 1-1/2 cups water.
2. 2-1/2 cups chicken or beef broth(omit salt).
3. 1-1/2 cups ginger ale and 1 cup of water.

Add to rice while cooking (one or more):
     A handful of raisins
     Chopped nuts
     Chopped onions, chives or shallots
     Half can of peas
     Chopped red or green peppers
     Chopped ham, salami or chicken
     Sliced mushrooms
     Diced smoked fish
     Sliced green or black olives

Rice Torino

1/3 cup butter or margarine
1-1/2 cups long grain rice
1 cup chopped onion
1 clove garlic, minced
1/2 lb. sliced mushrooms
1 cup dry vermouth

3-1/4 cups chicken broth
1 t. salt
Pepper to taste
1/2 cup grated Parmesan cheese
1 cup peas

Brown rice in 3 T. butter, add onions and garlic and cook several minutes. Add remaining butter and mushrooms, cook several minutes and than add broth, vermouth, salt and pepper. Cover and simmer 20 to 25 minutes until liquid is absorbed. Add peas in the in the last 5 minutes. Serve topped with cheese.

6 to 8 servings

Cajun Red Beans and Rice

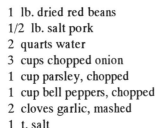

A good "old" standby from Louisiana.

1 lb. dried red beans
1/2 lb. salt pork
2 quarts water
3 cups chopped onion
1 cup parsley, chopped
1 cup bell peppers, chopped
2 cloves garlic, mashed
1 t. salt

1 t. each of black and red pepper
2 dashes Tabasco sauce
1 T. Worcestershire sauce
1 4 oz. can tomato sauce
1/4 t. oregano
1/4 t. thyme
1 lb. sausages, sliced
Cooked white rice

Soak beans overnight. Cook beans and cut up salt pork in salted water slowly for 45 minutes. Add vegetables, seasonings and tomato sauce. Cook over low heat another hour. Stir once in a while. Add sausage and cook another half hour. Serve over boiled white rice.

8 to 12 servings

NOTE: This dish is better warmed over, so make it a day ahead and just reheat.

Rice Milanese

1 cup rice	Pinch of saffron
2 oz. butter or margarine	1/2 cup grated Parmesan cheese
2-1/2 cups chicken stock	1 oz. butter
1 small onion, chopped fine	

Melt butter in sauce pan. Add onion and brown. Add rice stirring continuously. When rice has absorbed butter add the stock with saffron a little at a time. Keep adding stock while cooking without getting it to liquid. When rice is done, remove from heat. Add remaining butter and cheese and stir well.

4 servings

Risotto

This is almost the same as the above dish, just add a clove of garlic minced at the beginning.

Risotto with Chicken Livers

Sauté 1 lb. chicken livers in a little olive oil. Remove livers and make a gravy with some chicken bouillon and a little white wine and flour. Add livers and reheat. Serve surrounded by rice.

Variations

Add sliced mushrooms or olives to chicken livers while cooking.

Pilaf

Pilaf is cooked exactly as Risotto. Saffron or turmeric can be added along with celery, peppers, lamb, chicken or dried fruit such as raisins.

Arroz con Pollo

This Spanish-Cuban dish is rice cooked as Pilaf with a good pinch of saffron added when the chicken broth is added. Add sautéed cut-up chicken and five minutes before the dish is cooked, add a can of peas (pigeon peas are used in most of the Caribbean).

A Spanish chef will tell you that the chicken must be marinated in lemon juice, olive oil and white wine for 3 to 4 hours and add a little tomato paste when frying the bird.

Chinese Noodles with Special Sauce

This is one of my brother Bill's** favorites.

For each 8 ounces of cooked egg noodles make the following sauce:

3 T. Oriental sesame oil*	1 T. Oriental hot oil*
4 T. soy sauce	1 t. Hoisin sauce*
3 T. rice vinegar*	3 cloves garlic, minced
1 T. sugar	Ground ginger to taste
3 T. Chinese sesame paste*	3 scallions, thinly sliced

Heat all ingredients until well mixed. Cool and pour over cold, rinsed noodles. Mix well. Serve cold.

* Available in Chinese grocery stores.

** Brother Bill has his own cookbook entitled, "Burp" by Bill Koneazny. Copies are available at 50 Campbell Falls Rd., Southfield, MA. 01259.

THERE YOU GO AGAIN! TOO MUCH BRANDY IN THE SAUCE.

Pasta Many Ways

There are thick cookbooks devoted to pasta recipes and there are as many opinions about cooking pasta as there are Italian mamas. I will not attempt to give you my recipes, but list some of the various ways to prepare pasta.

Pasta with tomato sauce - May include ground beef, pork, veal, onions, peppers, mushrooms, wine, chicken, oregano, sugar, rosemary, basil along with tomatoes. Parmesan cheese and hot pepper may be added at the table.

Pasta with chicken livers - To a half pound of hot spaghetti, add 1/2 pound cooked chicken livers, chopped and one pound of mushrooms that have been sautéed in olive oil.

Pasta with tuna - Heat some olive oil and add a couple of cans of tuna fish, drained. Add hot spaghetti and mix well. Sprinkle with grated cheese.

Pasta with garlic and oil - Mash or mince 2 or 3 cloves of garlic and salt and pepper in a good olive oil. Heat and add cooked spaghetti and toss well.

Pasta with Morney - Use Morney sauce to cover cooked spaghetti. Chopped pimento may be added.

Pasta Bagaria - To a half of pint of tomato sauce, add an ounce of ham, 1 t. basil, 1 oz. butter, 1 T. capers, 6 to 8 chopped olives and 6 oz. red wine. Blend in blender. Heat and serve with hot spaghetti.

Pasta with Pesto - Make pesto sauce by mixing in a blender, olive oil, garlic cloves, fresh basil, pine or walnuts and grated cheese. Pour over hot noodles or spaghetti.

Linguini with Seafood - Add chopped lobster meat, shrimp, scallops or clams to a white sauce or better yet, mornay or hollandaise sauce.

Linguini with Clams - Mix olive oil with 1/4 pound butter, 2 cloves garlic, some oregano, parsley, pepper and a dash of Tabasco, 1 can of minced clams or better yet fresh ones. Sauté. Add 2 T. flour and 1 cup clam juice. Heat and serve over pasta.
Ripe olives and scallions may be added.

Pasta Mt. Etna - Cook a small eggplant (chopped) in tomato sauce. Add a package of frozen spinach or one 1 lb. can drained. Add a little red wine and simmer about 30 minutes. Serve over pasta.

Fettuccine with Fennel - In a large skillet, cook onion and prosciutto ham. Add 2 bulbs fennel, 2 cans tomato sauce and cook 10 minutes then add 1/4 cup basil leaves and 1/4 cup Parmesan cheese. Add to 1 lb. cooked fettuccine.

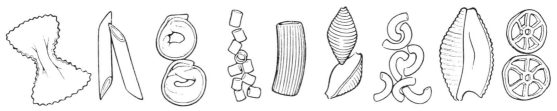

PORKO, HAVE YOU SEEN STALKY STRINGBEAN LATELY?

THE WAY THE BOSS COOKS, YOU'RE LUCKY YOU SEE HIM AT ALL. I THINK HE'S GAINED A FEW POUNDS JUST WORKING ON THIS BOOK!

Lasagna with Béchamel and Ham

Here's a different slant on Lasagna.

1 lb. cooked lasagna
2 eggs, beaten
2 cups thinly sliced mushrooms

2 cups ham, cut in strips
Boiling salted water
Béchamel sauce

Cook lasagna in boiling salted water with a little oil added until just done. While the lasagna is cooking, make the sauce (see page 19) and add eggs. Strain the lasagna and place a layer of pasta, half the mushrooms and ham and half the sauce. Then do another layer. Bake at 350⁰ for 20 to 25 minutes.

Variations

1. Use morney sauce instead of béchamel.
2. Use a can of cream of mushroom soup slightly diluted as the sauce.

Hamburg Pizza Pie

This is an easy way to have pizza without getting involved in making dough, as the hamburger is the crust.

1 lb. hamburger
1 t. seasoned meat tenderizer
1 clove garlic, minced
1 8 oz. can good tomato sauce
1/4 t. garlic salt 1 onion, thinly sliced

1/4 lb. pepperoni, thinly sliced
1 6 oz. can sliced mushrooms
1/2 lb. grated mozzarella cheese
1/4 cup Parmesan cheese, grated
Oregano, thyme, tarragon to taste

Mix first three ingredients and put into a 12 inch pizza pan or baking pan. Mix next three items and spread over beef mixture. Then add onion, pepperoni and mushrooms followed by the cheese. Sprinkle with herbs and Parmesan and bake in a 450⁰ oven for 15 minutes.

This dish can be made in a stove top oven or an electric frying pan with fair results.

4 to 6 servings

Some Variations on Pizzas

The Americans have developed the Pizza far beyond the humble cheese and tomato pie that first came over from Italy. Now we have deluxe, four combo, Mexican, Chinese, Sicilian, Greek, German, Irish and many others.

Here are a few of the variations that you can use when building your own pizza.

Of course, they all should have tomato sauce and cheese. Now you can add:

Anchovies
Asparagus
Bacon
Mushrooms
Peppers
Onions
Sausage
Hamburg
Pepperoni
Salami
Sardines
Olives
Ham
Pimiento

Capers
Zucchini
Crab meat
Lobster
Shrimp
Frankfurters
Spam
Potted meat
Swiss cheese
Parmesan cheese
Cheddar cheese
Corned beef
Pastrami
Chili peppers

Corn Fritters

1 cup sifted flour
1 T. baking powder
3/4 t. salt
Oil for deep frying

2 cups cream style corn
2 eggs, beaten
1 T. sugar

Heat oil to 365°. Mix all ingredients and fry until light brown. Serve with syrup or powdered sugar.
6 to 8 servings

Apple Fritters

6 T. flour
1 T. oil
1 egg, separated
Pinch of salt

5 T. warm water
Sugar
Apple slices
Oil for frying

Mix flour and water together. Beat oil, egg yolk, salt and add to batter. Let mixture stand about one hour. Add beaten egg white. Roll apple slices in sugar, dip in batter and fry in hot oil. Remove when golden, drain and serve. If Apple is real tart, more sugar can be sprinkled on. Garnish with cinnamon.

Variation

Serve with sour cream.

In the Bahamas, the locals put in bird peppers...the hottest pepper known.

Conch Fritters

4 Conch
2 Onions
1 green pepper
Juice of 2 limes

2 cups flour
2 t. baking powder
Water
Salt and pepper to taste

Put conch meat through grinder or processor with chopped onion and pepper. Add lime juice and seasoning. Add flour, baking powder and water to make a loose batter. Drop batter from tablespoon into deep fat (2 inches deep). Cook until golden on each side.

Makes 15 to 25 fritters

Clam Fritters

1 cup sifted flour
1 pint clams, minced
Salt and pepper to taste

1 t. baking powder
1 egg, beaten
Oil for frying

Mix flour and baking powder together and add egg, clams, salt and pepper. Drop by spoonful into hot fat and deep fry until brown.

Rum Rice Fritters

1 cup rice, raw
2-1/2 cups milk
2 oz. brown sugar
1/2 t. vanilla extract
2 egg yolks

4 T. rum
1 egg
Bread for crumbs
Oil for frying
Grated Coconut

Cook rice in milk, sugar and vanilla until done, but firm. Beat egg yolks with rum and mix with the rice. Grease cutting board, dredge with flour and spread rice on board to 1/2 inch thickness. Chill in refrigerator about 20 minutes. Cut into 1 x 3 inch pieces. Beat egg, brush fritters and coat with crumbs.

Heat 1/2 inch of oil in pan or deep fryer until golden. Sprinkle with coconut.

4 to 6 servings

NOTE: See "Calas" for a different rice cake.

Crepes

For those who have never made them, crepes are much easier to make than you may have thought. Try and enjoy.

3 eggs, beaten	1/2 t. salt
2 to 3 cups flour	1 cup milk

Combine eggs, flour, salt and milk. Beat until smooth. Let stand 20 minutes. Pour 1/4 cup of batter into hot, lightly greased, fry pan and cook on one side only.

Dinner Crepes

Seafood crepes - Chop up some cooked shrimp, lobster, scallops, oyster or crab meat. Mix with white sauce, morney or other cheese sauce. Heat. Spread on pancakes, Roll and serve.

Easy seafood - Open a can of shrimp, crab meat and oysters, drain. Mix with a can of cream of mushroom soup and a little cheddar cheese. Proceed as above.

Crepes provincial - Cook 8 slices bacon until crisp. Sauté onions and pepper in a little bacon fat. Add mushrooms, bacon and 1-1/2 cups sharp cheddar cheese. Put a couple of ounces of cheese mixture on each crepe. Roll crepes and put in a baking dish. Top with tomato sauce. Bake at 350⁰ for 15 minutes. Top with 1/2 cup shredded cheese and return to oven until melted.

Chicken crepes - Add one cup of chopped chicken (or turkey or tuna) to some condensed cream of chicken soup. Add a little chopped pimiento and proceed as above.

Spinach crepes - Mix half to one can cream of mushroom soup, 1 can spinach, drained, one small can mushrooms, drained. Mix and heat and proceed as above.

Ham and Asparagus - Mix half to one can of cream of celery soup. 1 can asparagus, drained and one cup chopped ham.

You've got the idea, now invent your own!

Dessert Crepes

Make the crepes as above except replace one once of the milk with brandy and add 2 T. sugar to the batter.

Dessert crepes can be stuffed with many kinds of jam, put in a chafing. dish and flamed with some brandy for a real fancy dessert. Sprinkle with a little powdered sugar and serve.

BREAD & ROLLS

Here are a few bread recipes I have collected over the years.

I'll be the first to admit that baking is my weak point in the cooking game.. I have such a hard time following a recipe, always adding extra ingredients or trying substitutes that quite often the wife will come into the kitchen and show me how to do it right.

Quick and Easy Poppyseed Cheese Bread

1/2 cup chopped onion
1 T. margarine
6 oz. shredded sharp cheddar cheese
1 cup biscuit mix

1/3 cup milk
1 egg
1 T. poppyseeds

Cook onion in margarine. Mix 1/2 cup cheese and biscuit mix. Add milk and beat until stiff. Knead on a floured board 8 to 10 times. Put dough on bottom of 8 inch pie plate. Combine remaining cheese with egg and spread over dough. Sprinkle with onion and poppyseed and bake at 425^0 about 20 minutes. Serve warm.

6 servings

Sour Cream Cornbread

Try this one to bring corn bread out of the doldrums.

1 cup self rising cornmeal
1/2 cup creamed corn
2 eggs, slightly beaten

1/4 cup cooking oil
1 cup sour cream
Bacon grease

Mix cornmeal and oil. Beat in eggs then sour cream. Add corn. Grease heavy cast iron fry pan with bacon grease and pour in batter. Bake at 350^0 for 30 minutes.

Easy Cream Cheese Biscuits

1/2 cup butter
1 cup Bisquick

1/4 lb. cream cheese

Soften butter and cheese at room temperature. Mix with Bisquick and roll out thin on well floured board. Cut biscuits in about 1-1/2 inch size and bake until brown about 1/2 hour at 350⁰.

Pressure Cooker Bread

One recipe that I tried, called for 1-1/2 cups of sea water. This bread was so salty that we couldn't eat it. Other recipes call for 1/3 sea water and 2/3 fresh which should be about right. If you use the sea water, of course don't add salt.

1-1/2 cups water
1 packet dried yeast
1-1/2 T. salt
4 cups flour

1-1/2 T. sugar
Shortening or margarine
Cornmeal or wheat germ

Dissolve yeast in warm water (not hot water as it will kill the yeast) for about 5 minutes. Add salt and sugar then stir in flour. Let rise from 1-1/2 to 2 hours. Remove rubber gasket from pressure cooker and grease well. Sprinkle cornmeal or wheat germ in pot and add dough. Cover and cook over low heat for about 30 minutes. **DO NOT CLOSE PRESSURE VALVE.** Turn loaf and cook another 20 to 30 minutes.

Variations

1.   Add grated cheese or onions, chopped
2.   Use honey in place of sugar
3.   Add some caraway, sesame or dill seed or weed.

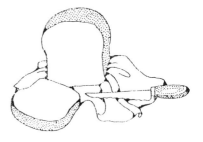

Quick Loaf Bread

Here is a quick and easy bread to make. We really "pig it down" when it is still hot from the oven. Just can't help ourselves!

2-2/3 cups lukewarm water
2 envelopes dry yeast
5 t. honey (or sugar)

6-1/2 to 7-1/2 cups unbleached
    bread or all-purpose flour
2 t. salt

Put water, yeast and honey in large bowl. Stir. Let stand 5-10 minutes until yeast foams. Stir in 3 cups of flour and the salt until smooth. *Gradually* add the remaining flour a cup at a time to make a soft dough.

Turn out on a floured board and knead lightly about 4 minutes. Place in an oiled bowl and rotate to coat dough with a light film of oil. Cover and let rise in a warm place until double in bulk (about 30 minutes). Punch down dough, divide in half and put into 2 greased bread pans. Cover and let rise again. Bake at 375° for 35 to 40 minutes or until done.

Makes 2 loaves

Beer Bread

In the previous recipe replace the water with luke warm beer. Dark beer or ale is best. Add 1 t. caraway seed and 1/2 t. garlic powder and replace the 2-1/2 cups of the white flour with unsifted rye flour.

Oat Bran Bread from Theresa Decker

5 packages yeast   1 T. sugar
1/2 cup luke warm water

Mix all together in bowl and let stand 5 to 10 minutes until yeast foams.
Mix in a separate large bowl:

6 cups boiling water   1/2 cup molasses
3 cups oats   1 cup honey
1 cup cracked wheat   1 T. oil
1 cup bran or wheat germ   1 T. salt

Let above sit until luke warm. Then mix in the yeast, water and sugar and gradually add 4 cups of unbleached white flour and 4 cups of wheat flour. Add more flour in equal amounts if needed, a little at a time, until soft. Put on a floured board and knead until all is mixed well. Place in an oiled bowl and rotate to coat dough with oil. Cover and let rise in a warm place. (I use the microwave) Punch down and divide dough into 5 loaves and place in loaf pans. Cover and let rise again. Bake at 375⁰ for 40 minutes or until done.

Makes 5 loaves

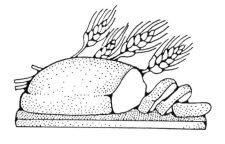

Sourdough Starter

1 envelope dry yeast   2 cups lukewarm water
1 T. sugar   2 cups unbleached bread
                                        or all-purpose flour

In a bowl combine yeast, sugar and water. Mix until yeast is dissolved and mixture is smooth. Stir in flour. Let stand at room temperature between 48 and 72 hours. If starter doesn't have a distinct odor keep it out longer. The stronger it gets the better the bread. Cover loosely and keep in refrigerator.

Dottie's Famous Sourdough French Bread

1-1/2 cups Sourdough Starter, at room temperature
3 cups lukewarm water
9-1/2 to 10-1/2 cups unbleached bread or all-purpose flour
2 envelopes dry yeast

5 t. salt
Butter or oil for pans

In a large bowl, combine the Sourdough Starter, 1-1/2 cups of the water and 1-1/2 cups of the flour. Stir until well blended. Cover and set aside in a warm place until bubbly, 30 minutes to 1 hour.

Add the remaining 1-1/2 cups lukewarm water and the yeast and stir until blended. Let stand until bubbly, about 5 minutes.

Stir the salt into 4 cups of the flour and mix it thoroughly into the dough. Gradually mix in the remaining flour, 1 cup at a time, until dough is soft but not sticky.

Turn out the dough onto a lightly floured surface and knead for 5 minutes, using as little additional flour as possible to prevent sticking. Place dough in an oiled bowl and turn to coat with a light film of oil. Cover and let rise in a warm place until doubled in bulk, 1 to 1-1/2 hours.

Punch down dough and place on a lightly floured surface. Divide into 4 equal pieces and cover loosely with a dish towel and let rest for 10 minutes.

Butter baking pans and or cookie sheet. Divide 2 of the quarters in half and roll into four 16-inch long ropes. Shape the other 2 into round or braids. Place them all in the baking pans. Cover and let rise in a warm place until doubled in bulk, about 1 hour. Preheat oven to 425⁰.

Slash the loaves on top with a razor blade or *very* sharp knife. Mist the loaves with cold water. Bake for 30 minutes, until crusty and brown. Let cool on racks before slicing.

Makes 4 long thin loaves and 2 round or braided loaves.

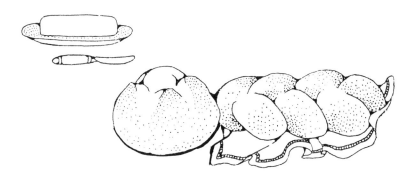

DESSERTS

Calas,
New Orleans Rice Cakes

I had these cakes in a little restaurant in New Orleans during World War II (the big one), when I was just a lad. I never forgot them and awhile ago I ran into the recipe and will pass it on.

1/2 cup rice
3 cups water
3 eggs, lightly beaten
1/2 cup sugar
3 T. flour

1/2 cake or package yeast
1/2 t. nutmeg
Oil for deep frying
Powdered sugar (optional)

Cook rice in 3 cups boiling water. Cook until soft and mushy. Cool, drain. Mash and mix with yeast that has been dissolved in 1/2 cup of warm water. Let rise overnight. The next morning, beat eggs and mix with rice. Add sugar and flour. Beat to a thick batter. Let rise for 15 minutes. Add nutmeg and mix well. Drop by spoonful in deep fat. If a fry pan or sauce pan is used, have about 2 inches of fat. Drain and sprinkle with powdered sugar, if desired.

Eggnog Fudge

2 cups sugar
1 cup of eggnog
1 T. corn syrup
4 T. butter

1 t. vanilla
1/2 cup chopped walnuts
2 T. semi-sweet chocolate pieces

Butter 3 quart sauce pan. Combine sugar, eggnog and corn syrup. Cook over medium heat stirring constantly until mixture boils., Cook to soft ball stage (238°) stirring only as necessary. Remove from heat and cool to lukewarm without stirring. Add 2 T. butter and vanilla. Beat until fudge becomes very thick and starts to loose its gloss. Stir in nuts. Spread in a buttered 8 x 4 x 2 pan.
Combine chocolate and butter and heat over water. Drizzle over fudge.

Makes 1 pound

In the fudge shops in North Georgia I have watched them make the fudge. When it was cooked it was poured on a large marble top table where it was cooled while mixing with a huge wooden paddle. This makes a better fudge, but I don't think it would work very well at home.

English Trifle - Sue Darcy

Trifle is another one of those dishes that can be made many ways. Here's one from an English lass.

1 pound of sponge cake
1 can peaches, sliced
1 can fruit cocktail
2 packages of instant vanilla pudding

1/2 cup sherry
1   3 oz. package Jello
Maraschino cherries
Ready Whip or whipped cream

In a large bowl or loaf pan, place drained peaches. Cut cake and cover peaches. Put drained fruit cocktail on top of cake. Then add another layer of cake. Make any flavor of Jello you wish and let it sit awhile. Pour sherry over cake. Pour Jello through cake. Refrigerate or cool to set. Make vanilla pudding as per directions. Put on top of trifle. Top with whipped cream and cherries.

Burnt Sugar Pudding

Here's an old Caribbean recipe that's easy to make.

8 ozs. brown sugar
1-1/4 cups boiling water
3 thick or 6 thin slices stale bread**
Pinch of salt
1/2 t. vanilla extract

2 cups hot milk
2 T. coconut rum*
3 eggs, beaten
Nutmeg

Melt sugar in heavy sauce pan until very dark. Add boiling water and simmer until syrup is thick. Remove crusts and cut bread into cubes. Butter (or Pam) a deep sided casserole or soufflé dish and cover the bottom with the bread. Mix vanilla and salt in hot milk and slowly pour over well beaten eggs. Pour caramel over bread, add egg, milk mixture and put dish in pan of hot water and cook in 375^0 to 400^0 oven until knife comes out clean. (approximately 30 minutes).
  *Coconut rum is optional. Almost any other liquor can be used if desired.
  **Stale bread can be made by putting in a slack oven for a few minutes.

Zabaglione

Here's an easy one that can be made on the spur of the moment. The only trouble is you will end up with 6 egg whites.

6 egg yolks
6 T. sugar

2/3 cup Marsala wine

Beat eggs with beater and gradually add sugar and wine. Place over boiling water and continue to beat until custard begins to thicken. Serve warm.

4 servings

Oranges in Marsala

6 large navel oranges
1 to 3 T. sugar

1/4 cup Marsala wine

Peel oranges and slice thin. Put in a dish and add wine and sugar. Cover and chill overnight.

8 servings

Bavarian Almond Cream

If you are not worried about calories and cholesterol and have a place to cool it this is for you.

4 egg yolks
5 T. sugar
Pinch of salt
1/2 cup of dark rum
2 cups heavy cream, whipped

2 t. gelatin
2 T. cold water
1/2 lb. almonds, blanched and finely
    chopped

Beat the yolks and sugar together. Add salt and rum and put in top of a double boiler. Cook and stir until it starts to thicken. Soften gelatin in cold water and add to pudding, stirring, then add almonds and chill until it starts to set. Fold in whipped cream. Put into individual cups or an oiled mold and chill several hours.

Taffy Pull Anyone?

The perfect answer to the rainy day when everyone has cabin fever and the kids are almost unbearable is, of course, a taffy pull.

 2 cups sugar
1/2 cup light corn syrup
2/3 cup water

1/8 t. salt
1 t. vanilla*
Butter or margarine

Grease a 9 x 9 pan or two 8 x 8 pans if two people will pull the taffy. Also grease a large surface for cutting the candy.

Cook sugar, syrup, water and salt until it will form a firm nearly brittle ball when tested in cold water (268˚). Stirring only until sugar is dissolved. Pour into greased pans.

When candy is cool enough to handle pour vanilla or other flavoring* in the center and fold over corners. Spray fingers with Pam and pull until candy is firm and white.

Stretch into 3/4 inch diameter long rope. Lay rope on greased surface and cut into pieces.

Separate pieces or wrap in wax paper.

* Spearmint, lemon or peppermint can also be used. Artificial colors can also be used.

Chinese Noodle Cookies

This recipe came off the noodle can. Here is a cookie that can be prepared on top of the stove.

2 6 oz. packs chocolate chips
2 6 oz. packs butterscotch chips

2 3 oz. cans Chow Mein Noodles
1/2 cup chopped nuts

Melt chocolate and butterscotch chips in saucepan over low heat stirring constantly. Remove from heat and stir in noodles and nuts. Dip out by spoonfuls on waxed paper. Refrigerate to chill.

Makes about 2 dozen

Sour Cream Apple Pie from Marlene Wood

2 cups apples or 2 apples
3/4 cups sugar
4 T. flour
1 egg, beaten

1 cup sour cream
1/2 t. vanilla
1/8 t. salt
1 9-inch pie shell

Arrange sliced apples into unbaked pie shell. Mix the remaining 6 ingredients together and pour over the applies. Bake at 350⁰ for 1 hour.

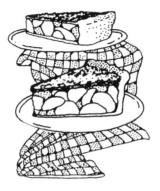

Topping:

1/3 cup sugar
1/3 cup flour

1/4 cup butter
1 t. cinnamon

Blend the above ingredients together and crumble this topping over the top of the baked pie. Bake for 15 minutes longer. Serve warm.

Serves 8

Canaan Depot Apple Pie

This pie was famous at the Railroad Station Restaurant in Canaan, CT. many years ago.
Make a regular apple pie with a top crust and cook until almost done. Take pie from oven and cut off top crust and place sharp cheddar cheese over the apples. Replace crust and cook for another 10 minutes or so until done.

Fayaway Cookies

Scrumptious delicious!

2 cups all-purpose flour
1/2 lb. butter or margarine
8 T. sugar or 9 brown sugar
2 T. vanilla

Coconut, grated or 2 T. coconut extract
Raisins and/or nuts, chopped
Blackberry brandy or
your favorite cordial

Cream flour and butter, mix in sugar, vanilla, coconut, raisins and / or nuts. Mix well. Add enough cordial to moisten and mix well again. Drop from a spoon on a foiled ungreased cookie sheet and bake in a 350^0 oven for 15 to 20 minutes.

Makes about 2 dozen

Variations

1.   Add chopped dates instead of raisins.
2.   Substitute fresh grated orange rind for coconut.

Hot Spiced Fruit

This makes a fine accompaniment for ham or chicken.

1 can of fruit salad or fresh, diced
1 jar of watermelon pickles

6 chopped gerkins
1/4 t. allspice

Combine all ingredients in saucepan with syrup from fruit salad and watermelon. Bring to a boil and serve hot.

Quick Fruit Desserts

1.   Soak melon balls in Amaretto and sprinkle with pecans or walnuts, chopped fine.
2.   Boil up the juice from a can of pears with some cloves and port or Marsala wine for about 10 minutes. Pour over pears and serve with sour cream.
3.   Use any fresh fruit that you have. Add a jigger of spiced rum for each serving. Top with whipped cream.

Sweet Potato Pie

Here's an old Southern favorite I picked up in my travels through Dixie.

2 cups cooked mashed sweet potato
1 T. grated nutmeg
1/2 t. cinnamon
1 cup sugar
1 t. maple flavorings*

1 cup milk
1 T. butter
1 t. salt
1/2 cup chopped pecans

Mix potatoes, salt, nutmeg and cinnamon. Add butter and blend. Add eggs one at a time beating until well blended. Stir in milk and flavoring. Pour into an unbaked pie shell. Bake at 325⁰ for 30 minutes. Remove, top with nuts and return to the oven for another 15 minutes or until well set.

* If you don't have maple flavoring, use maple syrup in place of the sugar.

Zucchini Cake / Bread

2 cups sugar
3 eggs, lightly beaten
2 cups squash (peeled and shredded)
3 t. vanilla
1 t. cinnamon

3 cups flour
1-1/4 t. salt
1/2 t. baking soda
1/2 t. baking powder
1 cup oil

Mix first 5 ingredients together and then add dry ingredients to mixture. Divide into two loaf pans (greased). Bake at 350⁰ for one hour.

Makes 2 loaves

Cheese Cake

1 lb. softened cream cheese
1-1/2 cups sugar
4 eggs, slightly beaten
Juice of half lemon (1-1/2 T.)
1 t. vanilla

1/2 cup butter, melted and cooled
3 T. cornstarch
3 T. flour
1 quart sour cream

Heat oven to 325⁰. Grease a 9-inch spring form pan. With electric mixer, beat cream cheese at high speed. Gradually beat in sugar, then eggs one at a time. At low speed beat in cornstarch, flour, lemon juice and vanilla. Beat in melted butter and sour cream.

Bake one hour or until firm around the edges. Turn off oven and let pan stand for two hours. Remove and let cool for at least two hours. Refrigerate for at least three hours before serving.

Serves 12

Variations

1. Add 2 ozs. cognac (use 4 tablespoons less of sour cream).
2. Add rum extract.
3. I'm a purest when it comes to cheese cake so I don't believe in toppings of fruit, etc. but you can cover with berries, peaches, cherries, strawberries or whatever you like.

White Chocolate Cheese Cake

3 T. butter, softened
1 cup finely chopped walnuts
2 to 4 ozs. fine quality white chocolate, chopped
3/4 cup heavy cream
3 8 oz. packages cream cheese, softened

1 cup sugar
1/4 cup all-purpose flour
4 large eggs at room temperature
1 T. vanilla

Coat the bottom and sides of a 10-inch spring form pan with the butter, coat them with the walnuts and chill the pan in the freezer for *15* minutes. In the top of a double boiler set over barely simmering water melt the chocolate partially, add the cream, scalded, whisking, and heat the mixture, whisking, until it is smooth. Slowly beat in the softened cream cheese and sugar and whisk all together.

Beat the flour into the chocolate mixture. Beat in the eggs, 1 at a time, beating well after each addition, and beat in the vanilla. Pour mixture into the prepared pan and bake the cheese cake in the middle of a preheated 425⁰ oven for 20 minutes. Reduce the heat to 300⁰ and bake the cheese cake for 45 to 55 minutes more, or until it is firm in the center and a tester comes out clean. Turn the oven off and let the cheese cake cool in the oven for 30 minutes. Transfer the cheese cake to a rack and let it cool completely in the pan. Chill the cheese cake, covered, for at least 6 hours and up to 24 hours. Run a thin knife around the edge of the pan, remove the sides, and with the knife dipped in hot water cut the cheese cake.

Daryl Moore's Italian Cream Cake

1/2 cup margarine or vegetable shortening	5 egg whites
2 cups sugar	5 egg yolks
2 cups flour	1 t. baking soda
1 cup buttermilk	1 t. vanilla
1 cup chopped nuts	1 small can angel flake coconut

Cream shortening or margarine and sugar, add egg yolks and beat until smooth. Combine flour and baking soda and add alternately with buttermilk. Add vanilla, fold in coconut and nuts. Beat egg whites until stiff and fold in. Bake in three 8-inch layer pans. Bake at 350⁰ for 25 minutes or until done.

Frosting

1 8 oz. package cream cheese	1/4 cup margarine
1 lb. confectioner's sugar	1 t. vanilla

Beat until smooth. Frost top and sides, sprinkle nuts on top of cake.

Raspberry Horseshoe's from Daryle Moore

2 cups flour	1/2 lb. butter or margarine
1/2 lb. cottage cheese	Raspberry jam

Blend flour, cheese and margarine and form into roll. Refrigerate overnight. Cut roll into 1/3 rounds and slice about 1/4 inch thick. Roll on floured board until thin. Cut into quarters. Put spoonful of raspberry jam into corner and roll like crescent. Pinch ends and shape into horseshoe on ungreased cookie sheet. Bake at 375⁰ 10 minutes or until light brown.

Almond Nut Squares

1 cup pecans or almonds	1/3 t. salt
1 cup brown sugar	1/4 t. baking soda
1 large egg	1 t. almond flavoring
5 heaping T. flour	Powdered sugar to cover

Beat egg, add sugar. Mix flour, salt, baking soda and sift into egg mixture. Add almond flavoring. Pour into a well greased 8 inch pan. Bake in 350˚ oven for 20 minutes. Sprinkle with powered sugar. Cut when cool.

16 squares

Quick and Easy Oatmeal Wafers

3/4 cup butter	1/4 t. salt
2 cups brown sugar	1 T. vanilla extract
1 egg, beaten	2 cups Quick oatmeal

Cream butter and sugar. Add beaten egg, salt and flavoring. Beat well and add oatmeal. Mix and drop from teaspoon on greased cookie sheet. Cook 10 minutes at 300^0.

Don't eat until they cool or you'll burn the roof of your mouth!

Wacky Cake

1-1/4 cups flour	1 t. baking soda
1 cup sugar	1/2 t. salt
3 T. cocoa	6 T. melted butter or cooking oil
1 T. vinegar	1 t. vanilla
1 cup cold water	

Sift flour, sugar, cocoa, baking soda, salt into ungreased baking dish. Punch three holes in mixture. In largest hole pour shortening, in medium hole, vinegar, in smallest hole vanilla. Cover with 1 cup water, stir well with a fork and bake 25 minutes in a 350^0 oven. Frost in pan—too soft to remove.

Daiquiri Pie

1 package Jell-0 Lemon Pudding
1 package Jell-0 Lime Gelatin
2 cups Cool Whip, thawed
2-1/2 cups water

2 eggs, slightly beaten
1/2 cup light rum
1/3 cup sugar
1 baked 9-inch crumb crust

Mix pudding, gelatin and sugar in saucepan. Stir in 1/2 cup water and eggs. Blend well. Add remaining water and stir over medium heat until mixture comes to a full boil. Remove from heat, stir in rum. Chill about 1 to 2 hours. Blend topping into chilled mixture. Spoon into crust and chill until firm. About 2 hours. Garnish with extra Cool Whip and/or lime slices.

Key Lime Pie

Preheat oven to 375⁰.

Crust:

1-1/4 cups graham cracker crumbs
1/4 cup sugar

1/4 cup softened butter

Combine the crumbs, sugar and butter and mix with fingers until crumbly and well blended. Press into 9 inch pie plate. Bake 8 to 10 minutes, then place on a rack to cool.

Filling:

5 egg yolks
1 can sweetened condensed milk

1/2 cup Key lime juice
1 t. grated lime rind

Lower oven to 350⁰. Beat egg yolks until fluffy. Gradually add milk, juice and rind. Pour into the cooled pie crust and bake for 15 minutes. Remove from oven and prepare topping.

Topping:

5 egg whites
1/2 t. cream of tartar

1 cup sugar

Raise oven to 425⁰. Whip egg whites until frothy. Gradually add the cream of tartar and sugar, beating constantly to form stiff peaks. Spread the meringue over the pie, covering all the way to the edges to allow for shrinkage while baking. Bake for 5 to 6 minutes or until meringue is nicely browned. Remove to wire rack to cool. Serve chilled.

No-Bake Banana Pie

1/3 cup melted butter or margarine
1/4 cup white sugar
1/2 t. cinnamon
1 cup Kellogg's Corn Flake Crumbs
1 8 oz. package softened cream cheese

1 can sweetened condensed milk
1/3 bottle lemon juice
1 t. vanilla extract
5 medium size bananas
2 T. bottled lemon juice

In a sauce pan over low heat combine butter, sugar and cinnamon until bubbles form. Remove from heat, mix in crumbs then press this mixture around a 9-inch pie plate to form crust. Chill. Beat cream cheese until fluffy and blend in sweetened condensed milk. Add 1/3 cup lemon juice and vanilla, then stir until thickened. Line chilled pie crust with three sliced bananas. Turn filling the pie crust. Refrigerate two or three hours until firm. Cut two bananas into thin slices and dip into lemon juice. Top the pie with banana slices. Chill again or serve immediately.

Strawberry-Rhubarb Pie

1-1/2 cups sugar 3 T. quick-cooking tapioca*
1/4 t. salt
2 cups fresh rhubarb cut in one inch pieces

2 cups fresh strawberries, halved
2 T. butter
1 9-inch pastry shell

Combine sugar, tapioca, salt and fruits. Pour into an 9-inch pastry shell. Dot with butter. Place pastry over filling. Slit top and bake at 425⁰ for 45 to 50 minutes or until syrup boils with heavy bubbles that do not burst.
   * Use flour instead of tapioca.

Pumpkin Pie

Pastry for a one-crust 9-inch pie
3 eggs, lightly beaten
3/4 cup brown sugar, packed
1/2 t. salt
3/4 t. ground ginger
1 T. molasses (optional)

1/4 t. nutmeg
1/4 t. ground cloves
1-3/4 cups pumpkin, mashed
1-1/2 cups undiluted evaporated milk
1/4 t. cinnamon

Preheat oven to 425⁰ with rack near bottom. Prepare pastry shell with standing fluted rim. Brush with little of beaten egg and chill. Mix the remaining beaten eggs with all the other ingredients. Pour into prepared shell and bake until a knife inserted near center comes out clean, about 35 minutes. If served cold decorate with whipped cream.

6 to 8 servings

Variation

Instead of pumpkin, use butternut or acorn squash.

Oatmeal Cake from Gayle Wiens

This recipe came off the Quaker Oats box 20-plus years ago labeled "Lazy Daisy Oatmeal Cake". Men particularly enjoy it, and it is one of the few cakes that is not improved with chopped walnuts.

1/4 cups boiling water	2 eggs, slightly beaten
1 cup oats, regular (not instant)	1 t. baking soda
1/2 cup butter or margarine	1/2 t. salt
1 cup sugar	3/4 t. cinnamon
1 cup brown sugar	1/4 t. nutmeg
1 t. vanilla	1-1/2 cups flour

Add oats to boiling water, cover, set aside for about 5 minutes. Meanwhile, grease and flour 9 x 13 pan. In large bowl, put both sugars, top with butter, then hot oats and mix well. Add vanilla, eggs, spices and mix well. Pour flour in mound on top, add soda and salt to flour and mix with it, then mix all together. Bake at 350⁰ about 30 minutes or until it tests done with toothpick. If it pulls away from sides of pan, it's overdone.

Topping:

1 cup brown sugar	1 cup chopped walnuts
1/2 cup butter or margarine	1 cup coconut
2 T. cream or milk	

Melt butter, add rest, spread over hot cake and broil until bubbly and brown. Cake is excellent without topping which is very, very rich.

Apple Pudding

1-1/2 cups flour	5 T. Crisco
2 t. baking powder	2 T. sugar
1/4 t. salt	1/2 cup milk

Mix flour, baking powder and salt. Cut in Crisco with knife. Add sugar and milk, pour soft dough over apple mixture.

Mixture:

2-1/2 cups sliced apples	4 T. butter
2/3 cup sugar	1/2 cup water
1 t. cinnamon	

Mix ingredients and pour into buttered shallow pan. Cover with dough and bake 30 minutes in 350⁰ oven.

Sauce:

1/3 cup butter	1 t. vanilla
3 T. cream	1/8 t. salt
2 cups confectioner sugar	

Cream butter and add rest of ingredients and beat two minutes. Roughly pile in small glass dish and chill. Serve chilled.

SOME USEFUL
INFORMATION

Kitchen Know-how

1 pinch = 1/6 teaspoon
1 dessert spoon = 2 teaspoons
1 scant cup = 1 cup less 1 tablespoon
1 heaping cup = 1 cup plus 3 tablespoons
1 pound of nuts in the shell = 1/2 pound shelled
5 cups ground coffee 1 pound = 45 cups
1 square chocolate = 1 ounce
1 square chocolate = grated 3 tablespoons
1 ounce (I square chocolate) = 1/4 cup cocoa
1 cup raisins = 6 ounces
2 cups dried beans = 1 pound
1/4 pound cheese = 3/4 cup grated or 1 cup shredded
1 pound boneless meat = 3 to 4 servings
8 to 10 egg whites = 1 cup

Fahrenheit to Celsius

Fahrenheit	Celsius	Oven
212	100	Very slow
250	121	
300	149	
325	163	Slow
350	177	
375	190	Moderate
400	204	
425	218	Hot
450	232	
475	246	Very hot
500	260	

Weight and Measures and Conversion

When you know	You can find	By multiplying by
ounces	milliliters	29.6
milliliters	ounces	0.034

1 ounce = 2.9575 centiliters
1 pint = 0.4732 liters
1 quart = 0.9436 liters
1/2 liter = 50 centiliters or 500 milliliters
1 liter = 1.0567 quarts or 33.8 ounces
1 teaspoon = 60 drops or 1/3 tablespoon
1 tablespoon = 3 teaspoons or 1/2 ounce
2 tablespoon = 1/8 cup or 1 ounce
4 tablespoon = 1/4 cup or 2 ounces
8 tablespoon = 1/2 cup or 4 ounces
16 tablespoons = 1 cup or 8 ounces
2 cups = 1 pint or 16 ounces
4 cups = 1 quart or 32 ounces
16 cups = 1 gallon or 128 ounces

So long folks, I'm history! Hope I helped you on the weight. Mr. Birdseye is looking for me so I'm going into hiding.

Butter or Margarine:

        1 stick = 4 ounces or 8 tablespoons or 1/2 cup

        1 pound = 2 cups

Flour:

        1 pound white = 4 cups

        1 pound whole wheat = 3-1/2 cups

        1 pound cake = 4-1/2 cups

Rice:

        1 pound = 2 cups

        1 cup raw rice = 3 cups of cooked rice

Bread crumbs:

        2 ounces = 1 cup

Oatmeal:

        1 pound = 2-3/4 cups

Sugar:

        1 pound granulated = 2 cups

        1 pound brown = 2-2/3 cups

Potatoes:

        1 pound unpeeled raw potatoes = 2 cups mashed

        Use 1 to 1-1/2 t. salt per quart of liquid for cooking vegetables

Dinner Guest Log

You'll be surprised how handy this list will be!

* BR - Beer   G - Gin   RW - Red Wine   RY - Rye
WW - White Wine   V - Vodka   R - Rum   S - Scotch
           B - Bourbon   NA - No Alcohol

GUEST	NO RESTRICTIONS	LOW SALT	LOW CAL	LOW CHOLESTEROL	NO DESSERT	FAVORITE DRINKS*	BRAND/MIXER	FAVORITE FOOD	STEAKS: RARE, MED. RARE, MED., WELL DONE	REMARKS
EXAMPLE: Betty Smith		X		X		WW	Rhine	Anything but kidneys	MR	Always brings a dip
Burt Smith	X					V,S,BR	Tonic, Soda	No Limas	R	Loves Cheesecake

GUEST	NO RESTRICTIONS	LOW SALT	LOW CAL	LOW CHOLESTEROL	NO DESSERT	FAVORITE DRINKS*	BRAND/MIXER	FAVORITE FOOD	STEAKS: RARE, MED.RARE, MED., WELL DONE	REMARKS
			X		X	WW	Rhine	Anything but kidneys	MR	Always brings a dip

GUEST	NO RESTRICTIONS	LOW SALT	LOW CAL	LOW CHOLESTEROL	NO DESSERT	FAVORITE DRINKS*	BRAND/MIXER	FAVORITE FOOD	STEAKS: RARE, MED RARE, MED., WELL DONE	REMARKS
			X		X	WW	Rhine	Anything but kidneys	MR	Always brings a dip

LOG OF MEALS SERVED				
Date	Menu	Book Page	Variations	Critique
Place Guests				
Place Guests				
Place Guests				
Place Guests				
Place Guests				
Place Guests				

Date	Menu	Book Page	Variations	Critique
Place Guests				
Place Guests				
Place Guests				
Place Guests				
Place Guests				
Place Guests				

LOG OF MEALS SERVED

Date	Menu	Book Page	Variations	Critique
Place Guests				
Place Guests				
Place Guests				
Place Guests				
Place Guests				
Place Guests				

LOG OF MEALS SERVED				
Date	Menu	Book Page	Variations	Critique
Place Guests				
Place Guests				
Place Guests				
Place Guests				
Place Guests				
Place Guests				

LOG OF MEALS SERVED				
Date	Menu	Book Page	Variations	Critique
Place Guests				
Place Guests				
Place Guests				
Place Guests				
Place Guests				
Place Guests				

Index for Personal Recipes

Index for Personal Recipes

Index for Personal Recipes

About the Authors

Photo by Phyllis Dodge

Jack Koneazny, from Hartford, Connecticut, served in the U.S. Maritime Service and the Army during World War II, having spent over 2 years in the E.T.O. He spent 28 years in the reserves and worked as a tree surgeon until his retirement.

Dottie was born in Springfield, Massachusetts and for many years owned a boutique in Western Massachusetts.

They have traveled extensively on their sailboat, Fayaway, for almost twenty winters and have traveled throughout Europe and the Caribbean since their retirement.

Jack is now working on a book about his exploits during World War II. He is the author of *"Signal Hoists for Yachtsmen"* and numerous magazine articles on cooking and boating.

Index

GET MORE BOOKS FROM R & E AND SAVE!

TITLES	ORDER #	PRICE
Only The Best *Fantastic International Recipes With A Regional Flair*	051-X	$11.95
True Southern Family recipes... *You'll love it!* *Learn and enjoy great down-home cooking!*	922-9	14.95
The New Bachelor's Cookbook *The indispensable guide to your mysterious kitchen!*	955-5	7.95
This for That *Quick substitutions for foods and condiments for todays health!*	847-6	6.95
All American Cooking *The best recipes from across our nation!*	902-4	7.95

The Lowfat Mexican Cookbook
Simple low fat techniques without losing the flavor! 896-6 $6.95

Belly Laffs Beyond the Blender
You'll Share Hundreds of Jokes Heard and Told by
Comedian and Bartender Margo Guidry 843-5 6.95

The Newlywed Cookbook
Designed for novices in the kitchen! 877-X 12.95